Adult
Coloring Book
Relaxation & Stress Relieving Patterns

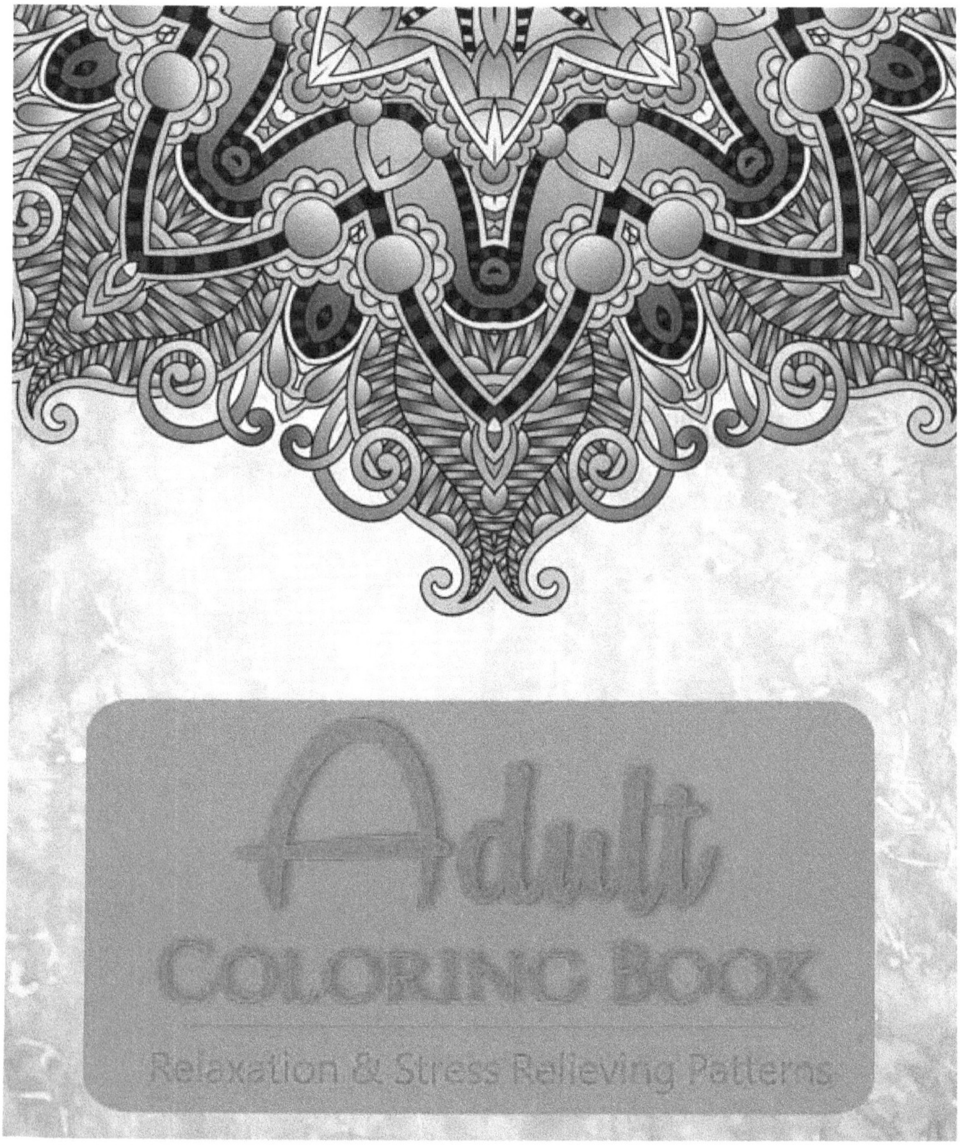

Vol. 1

V ART™

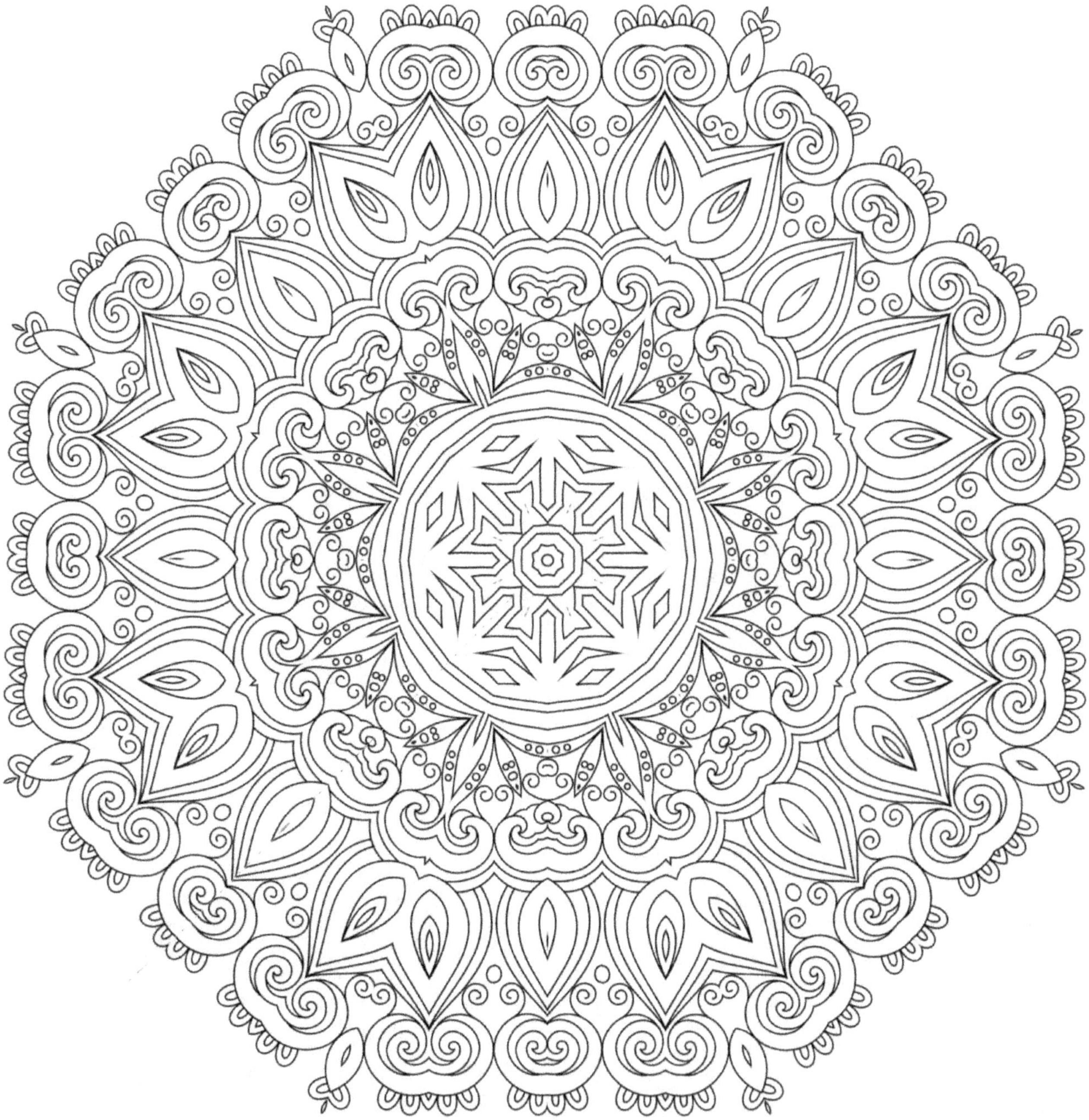

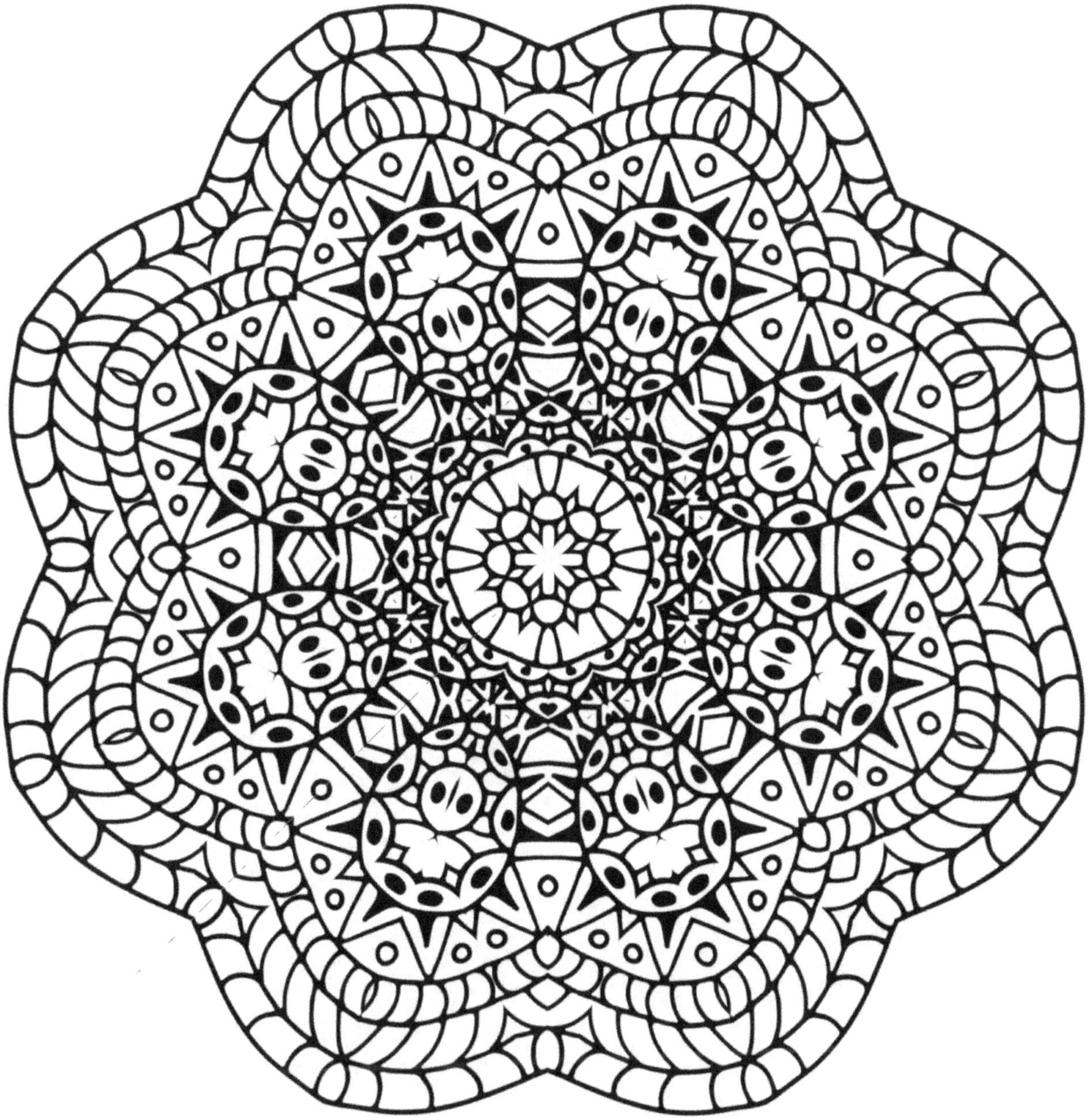

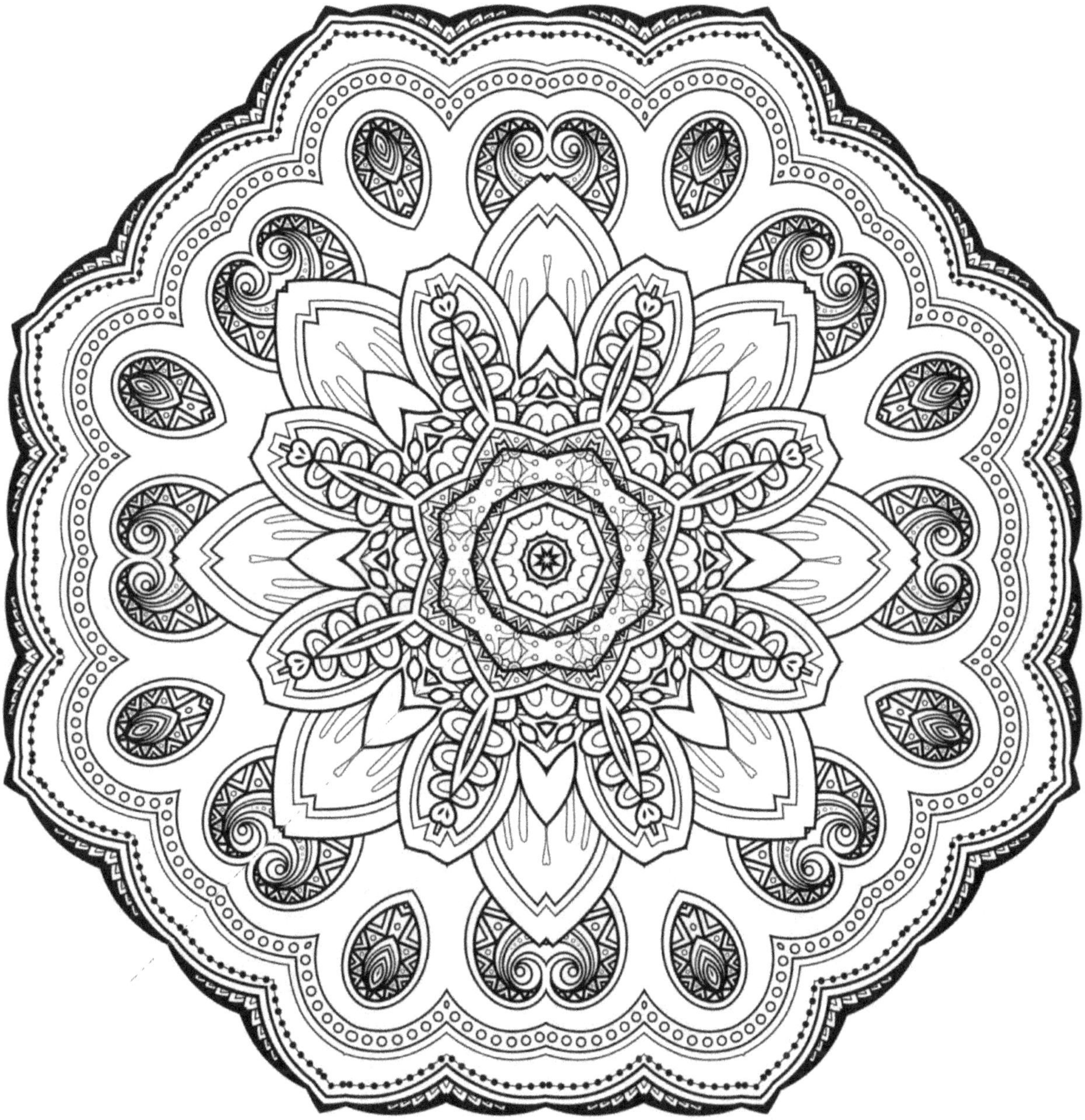

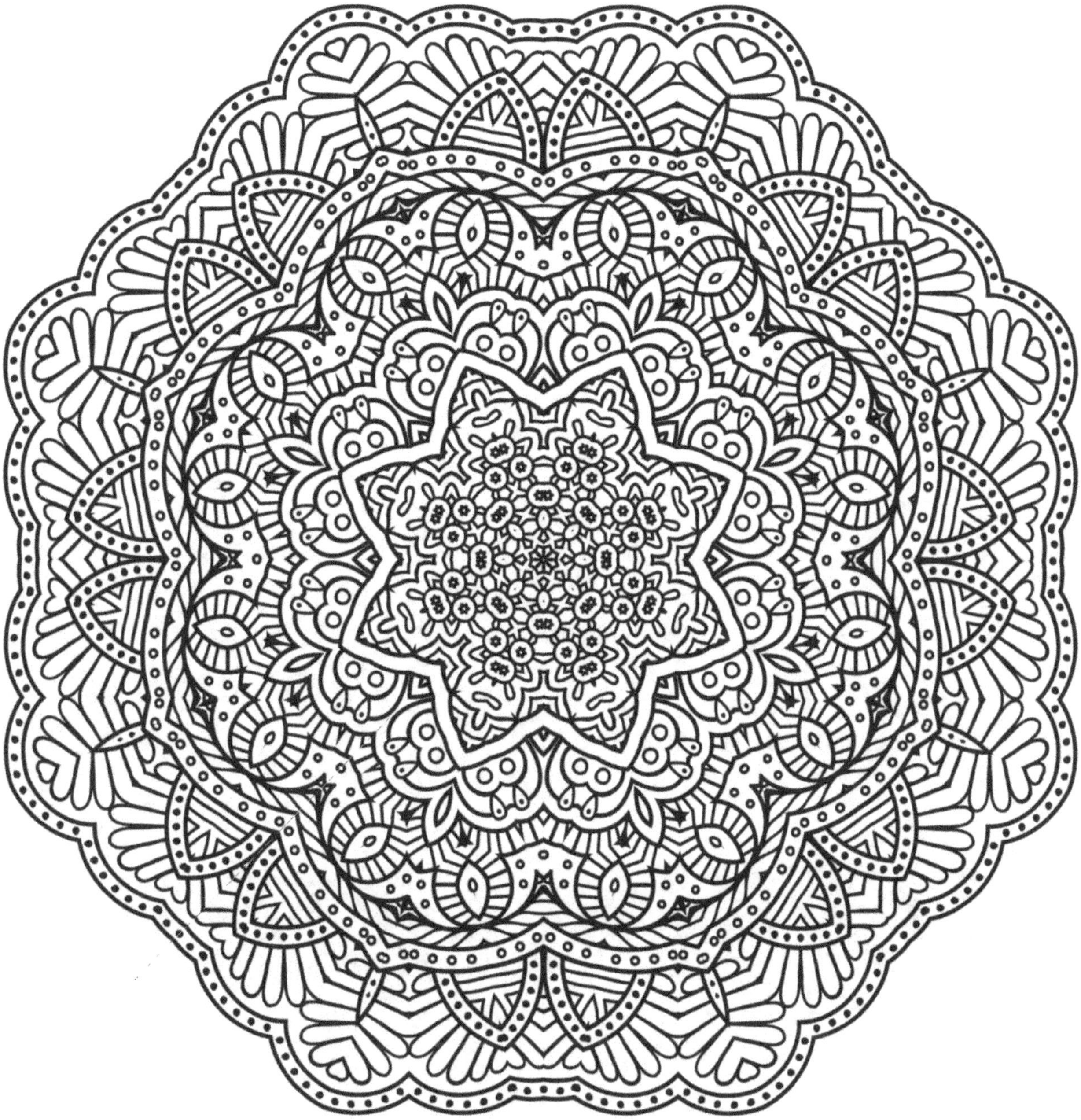

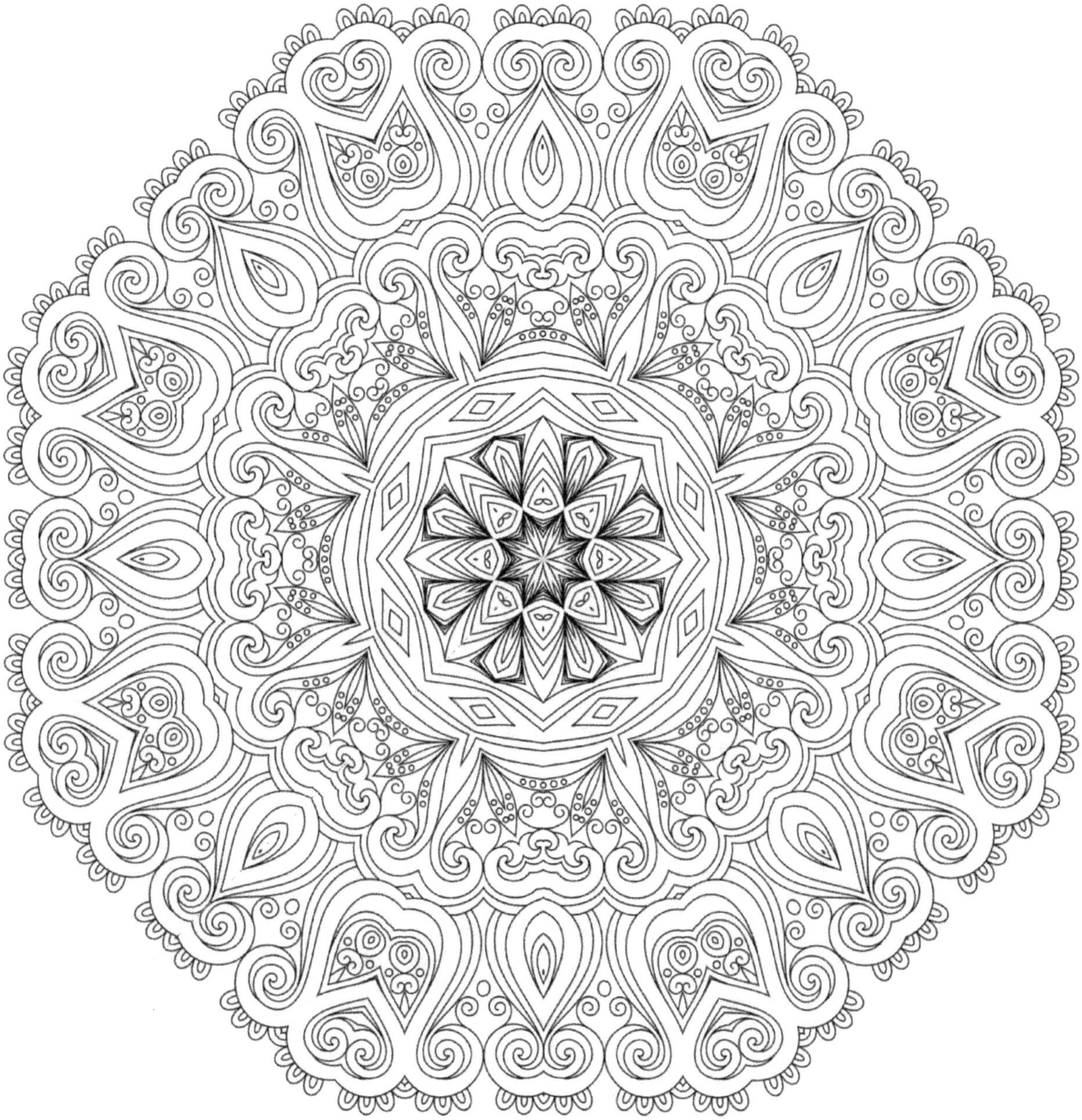

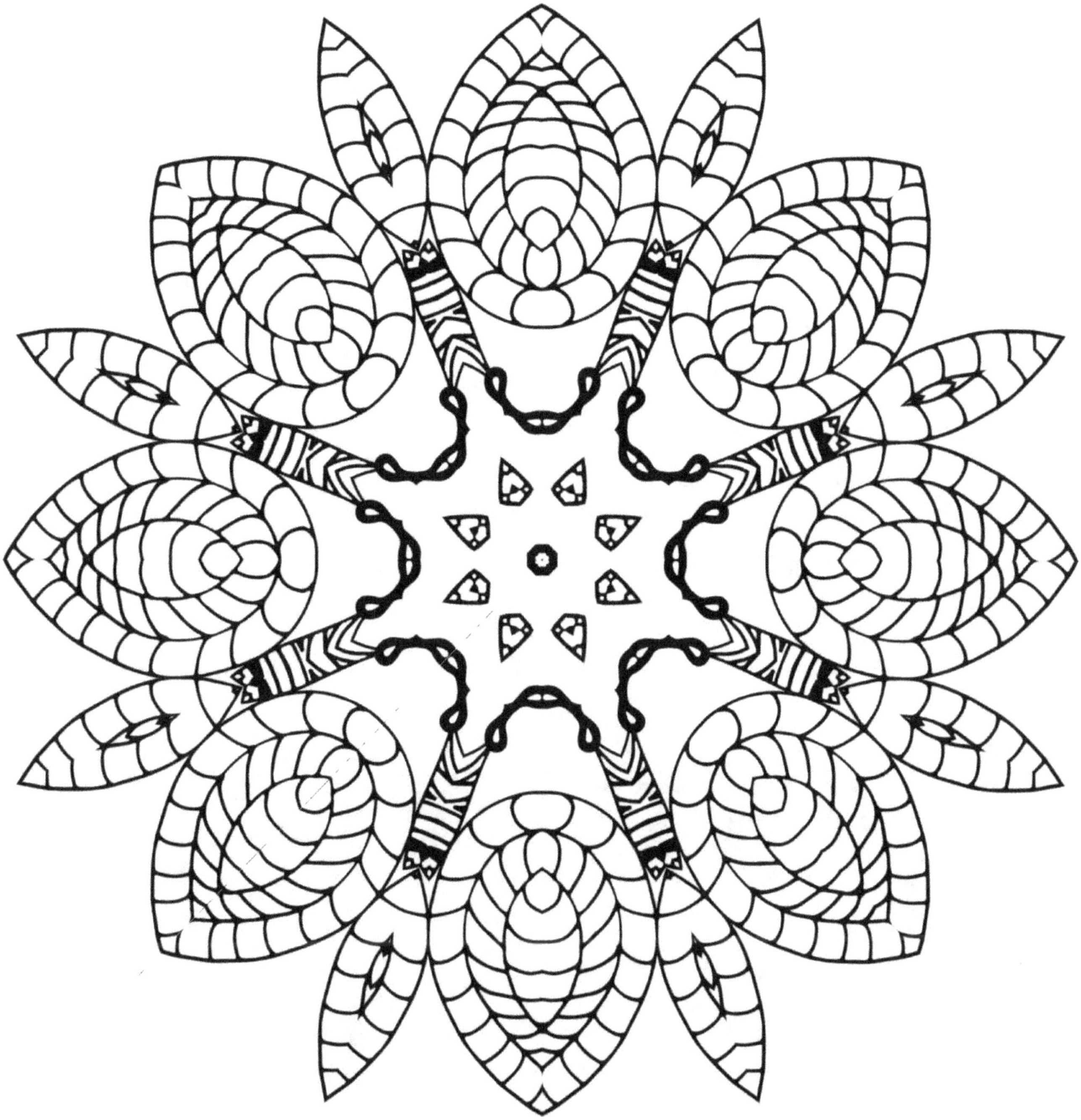

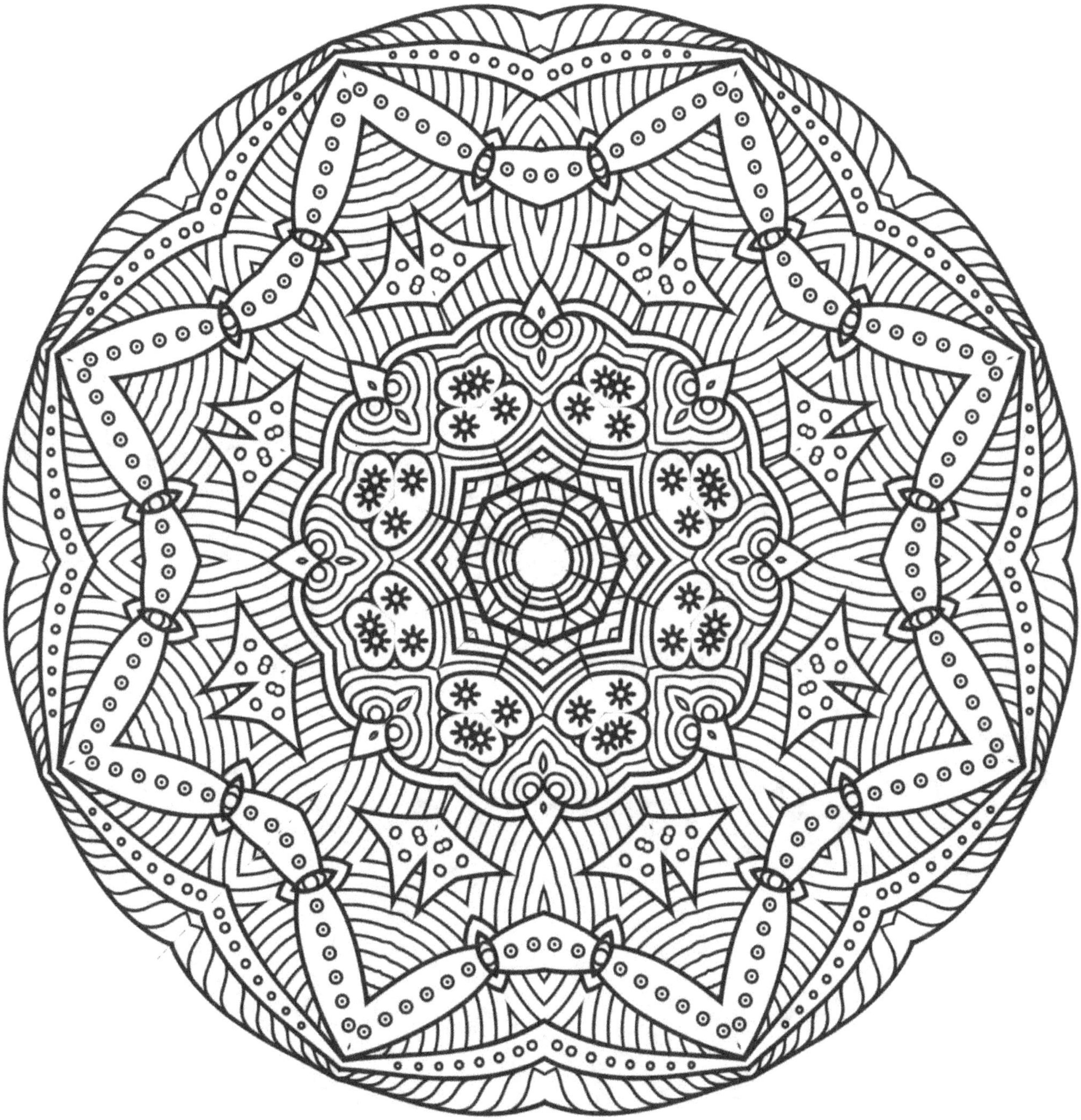

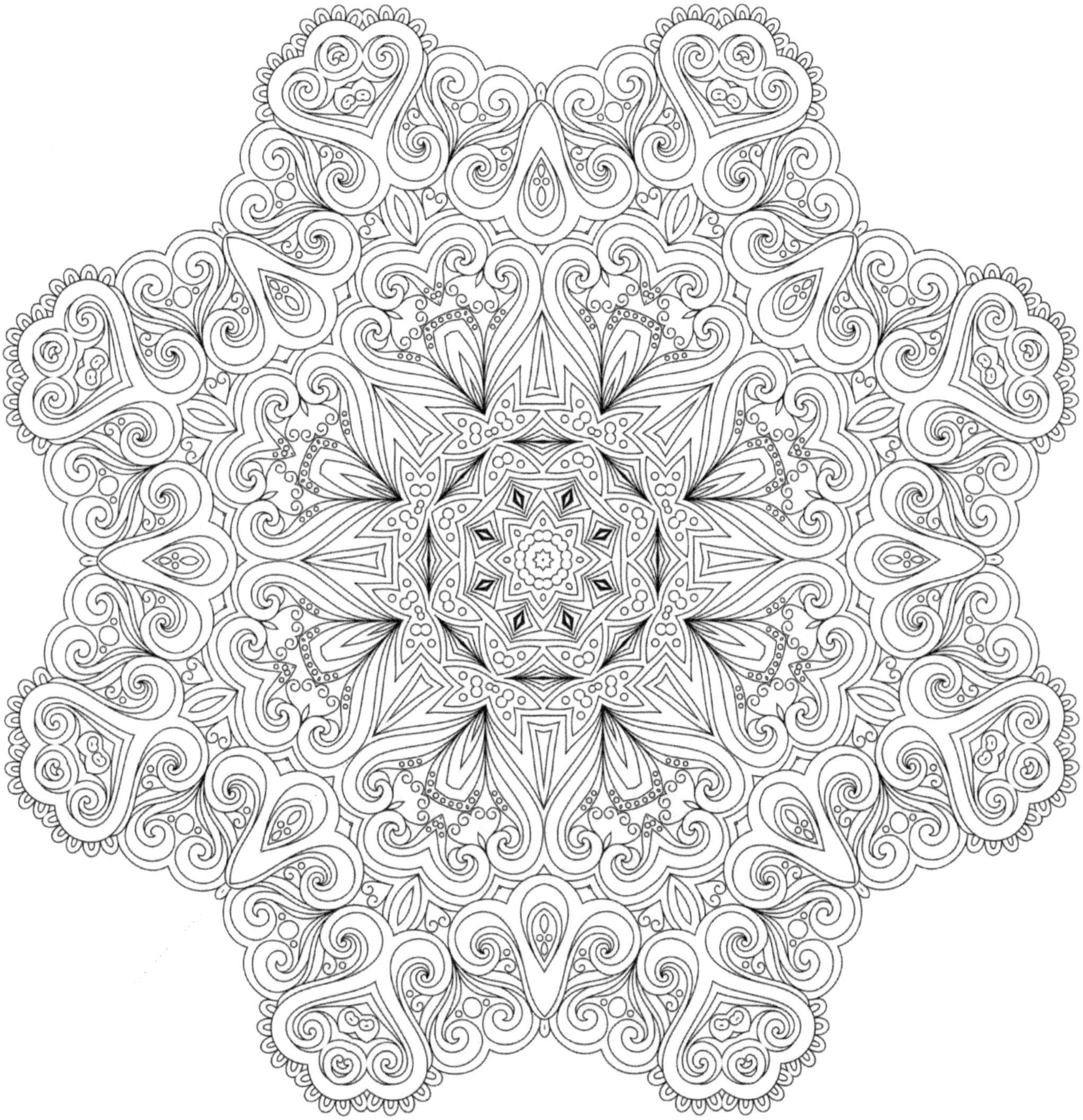

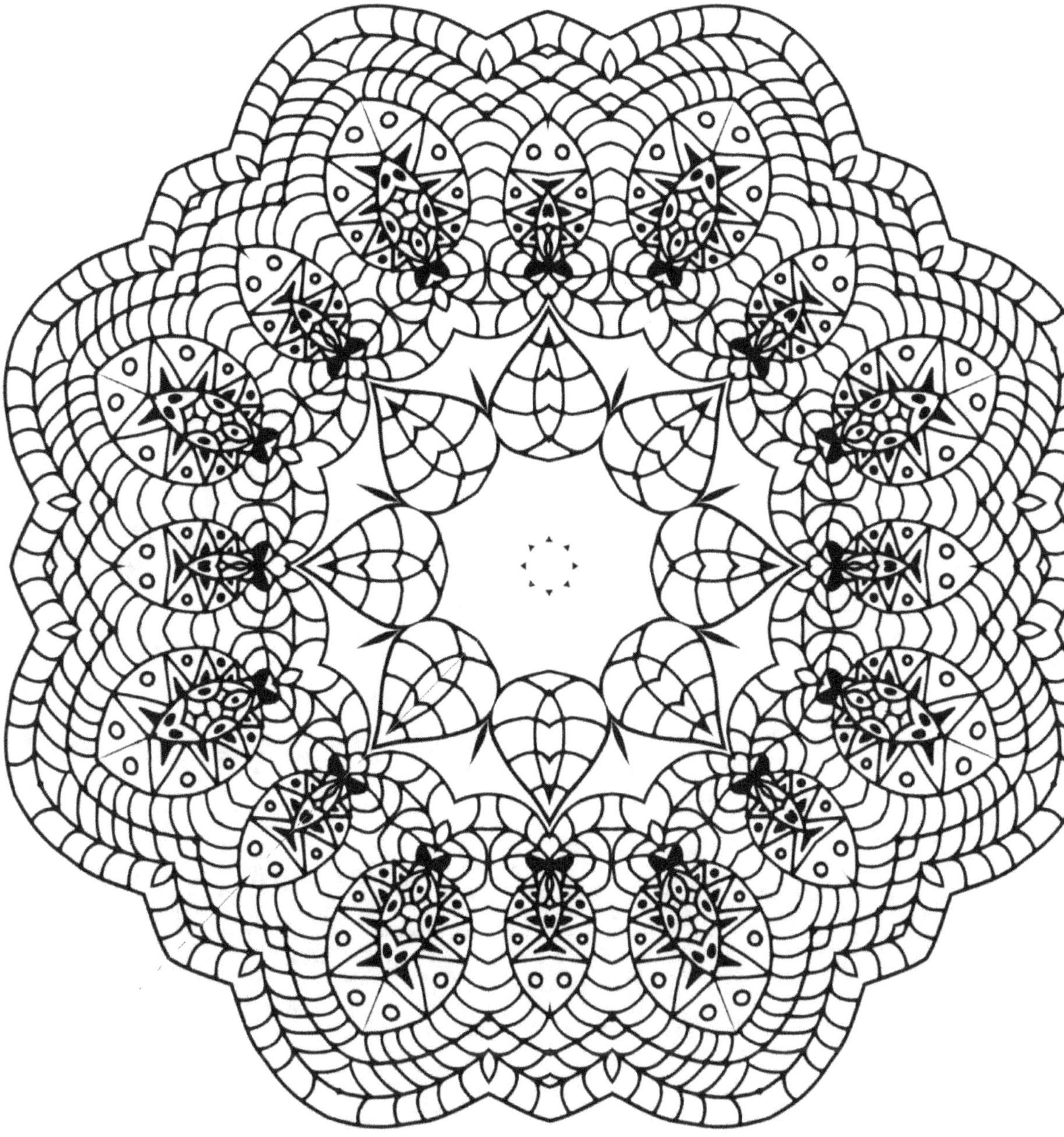

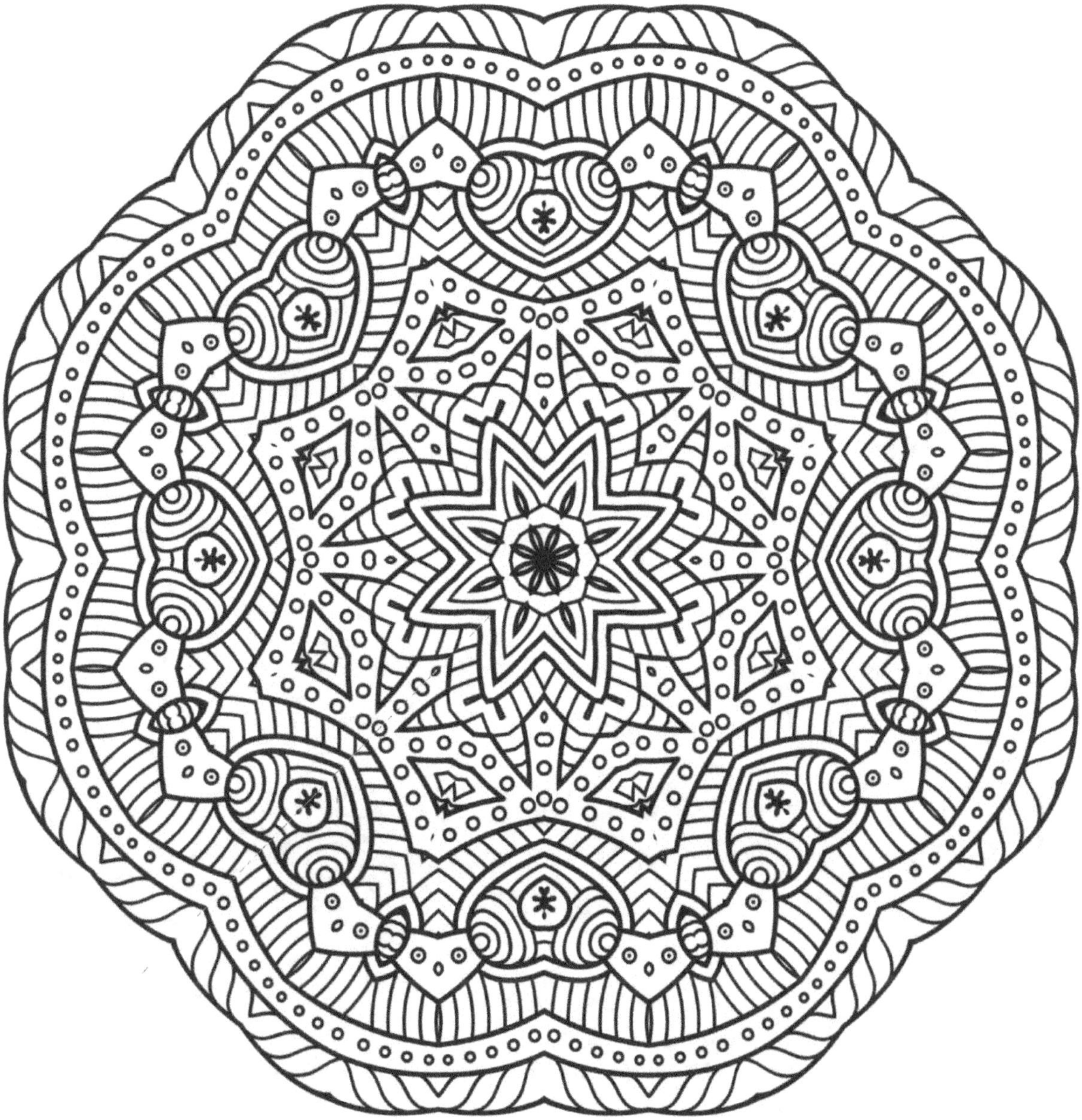

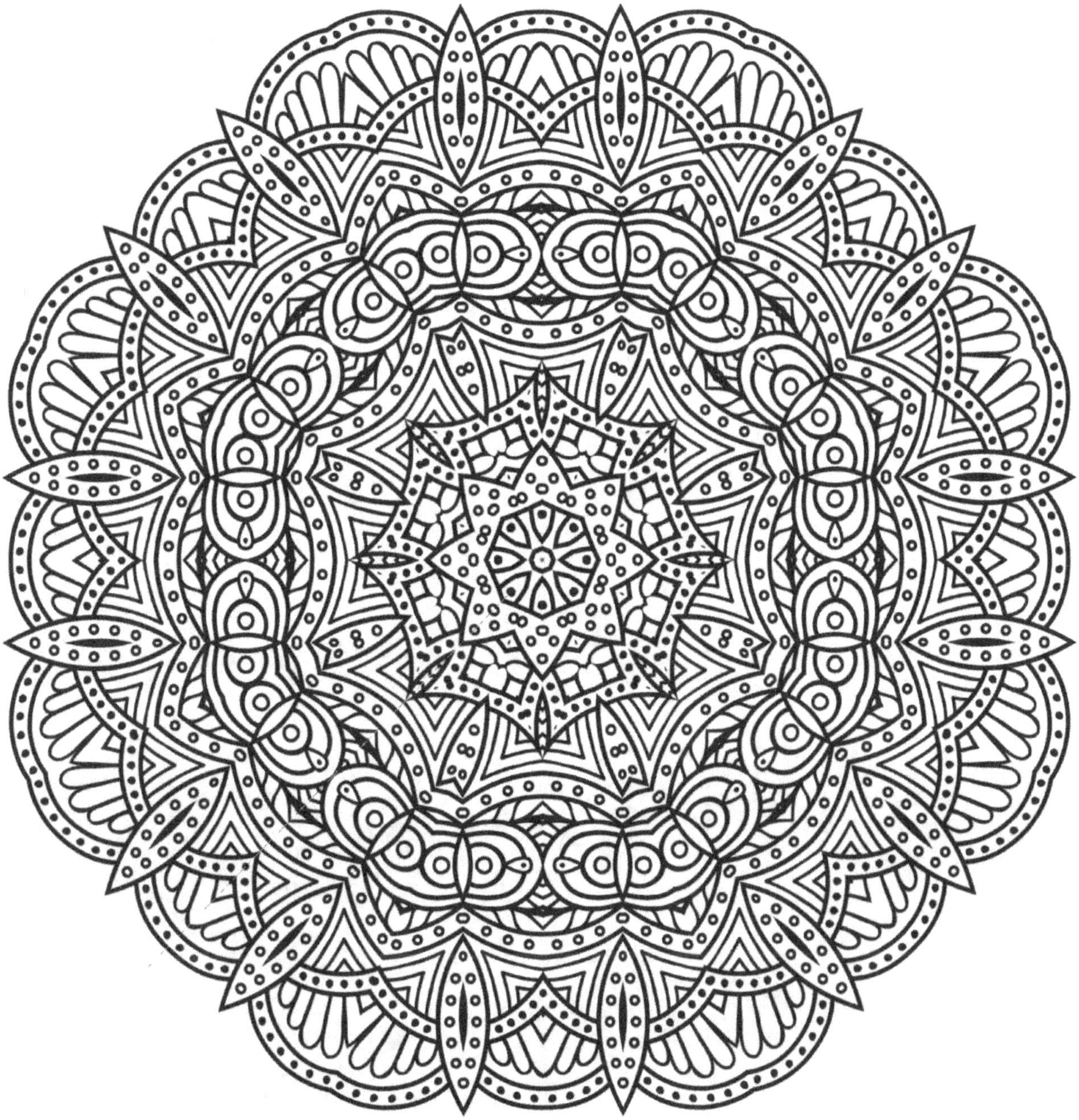

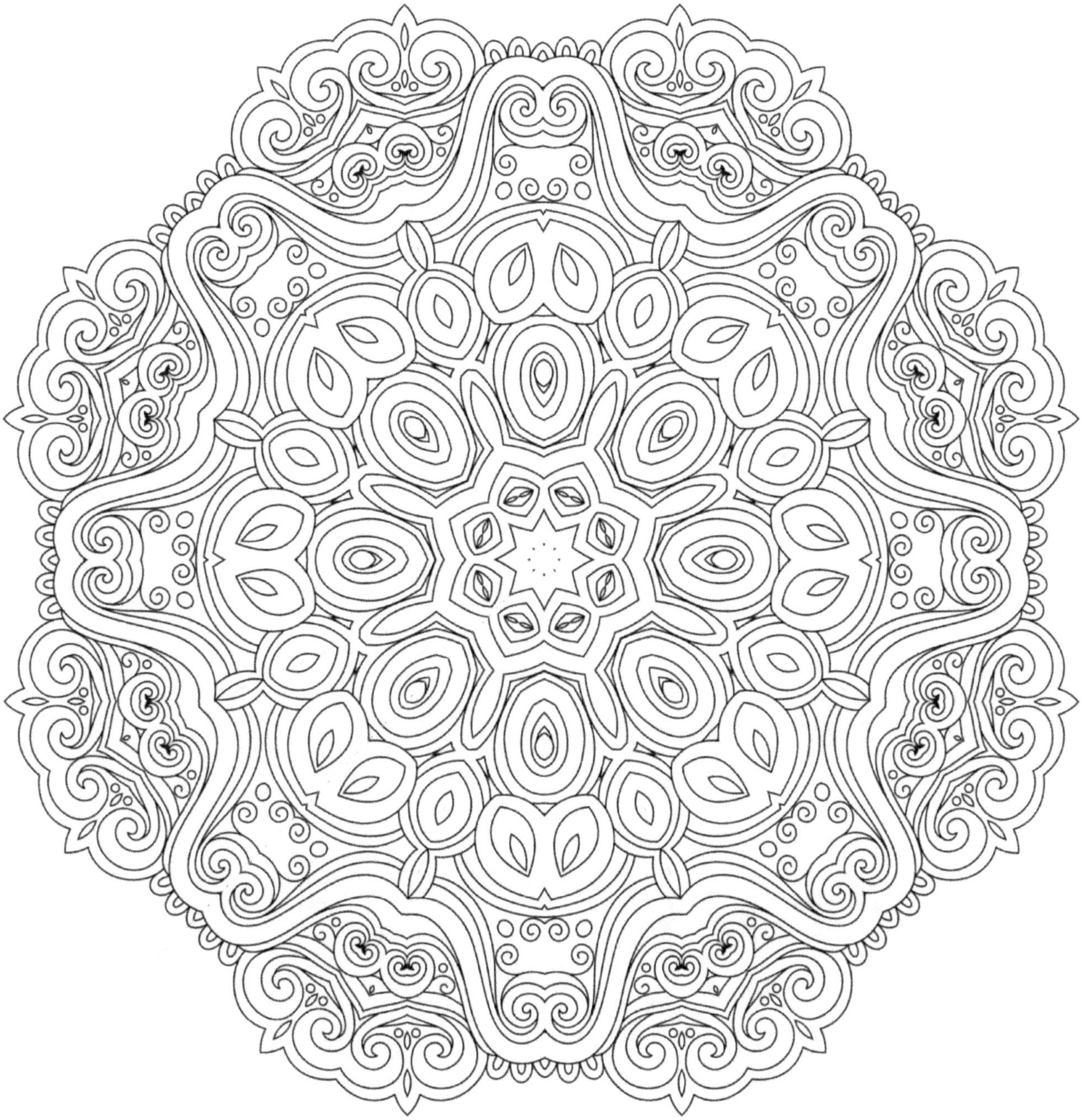

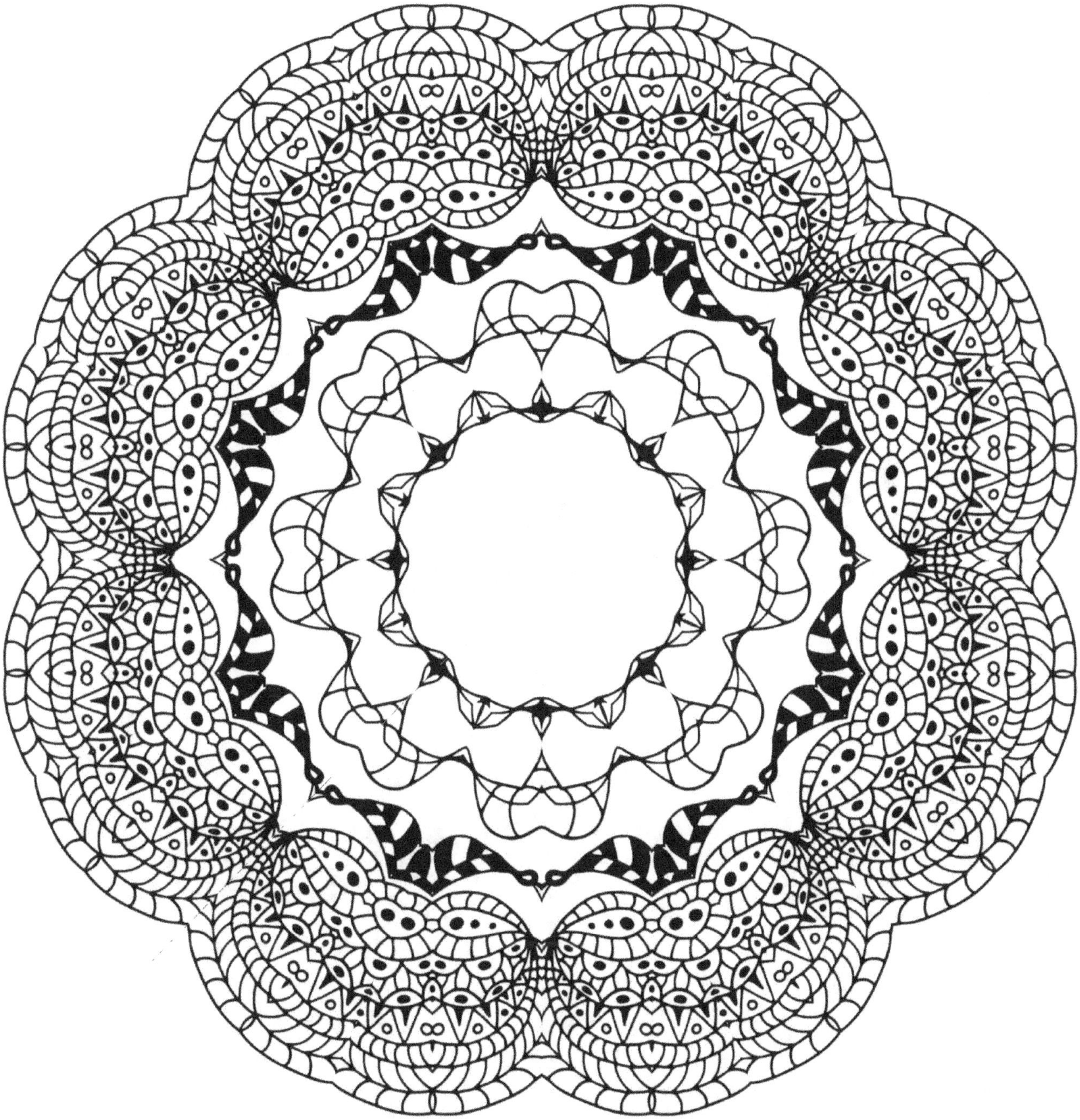

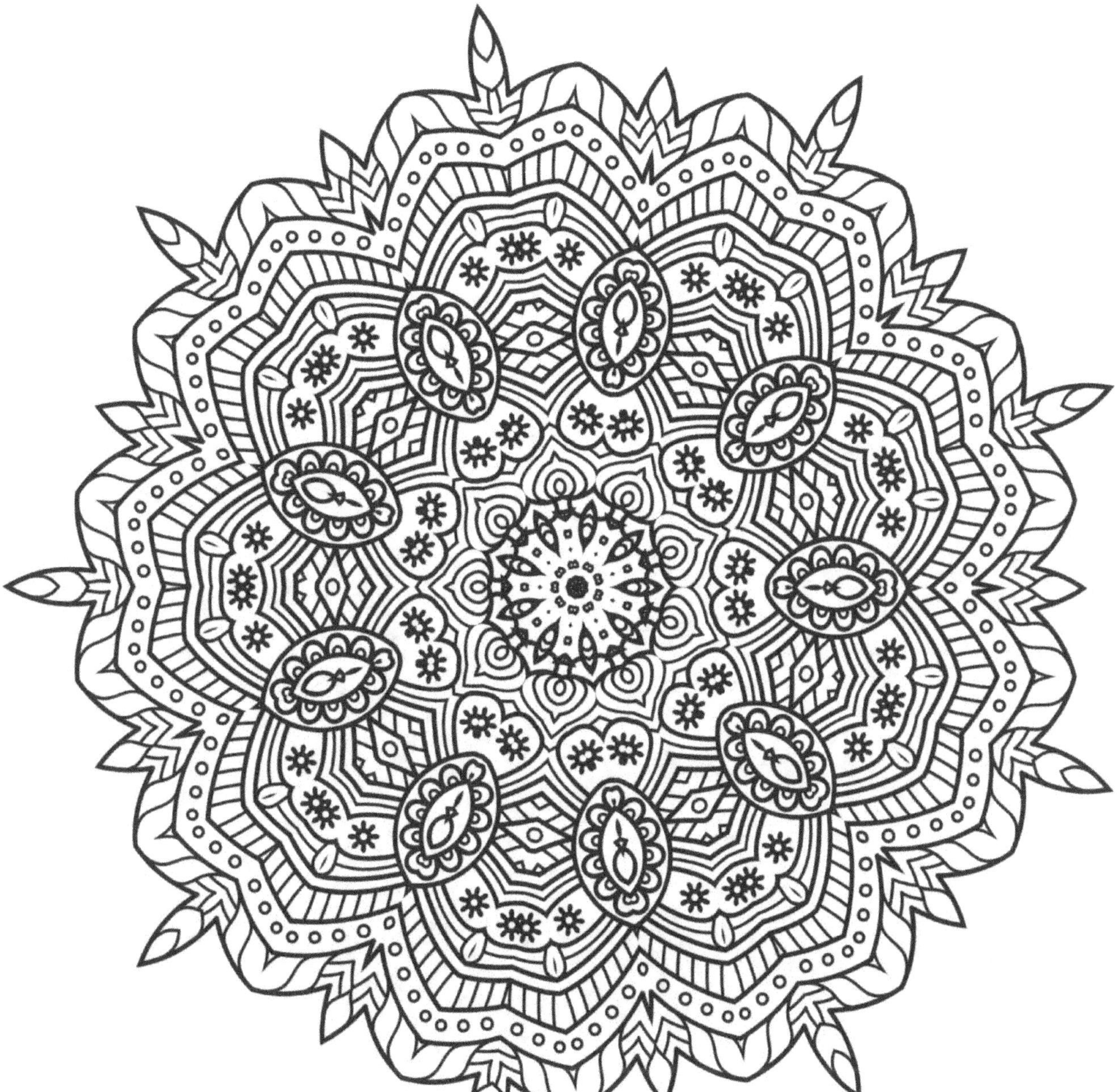

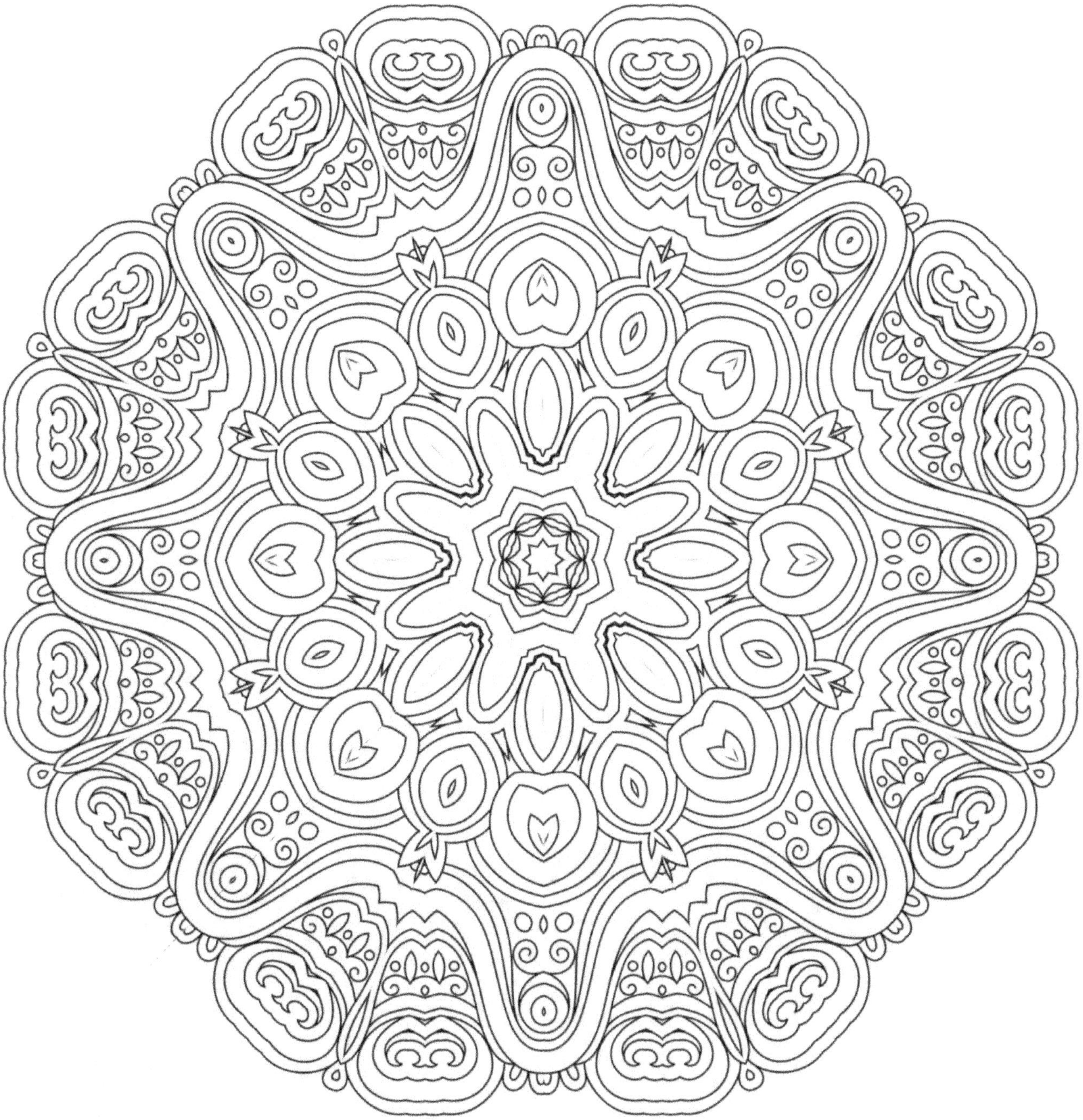

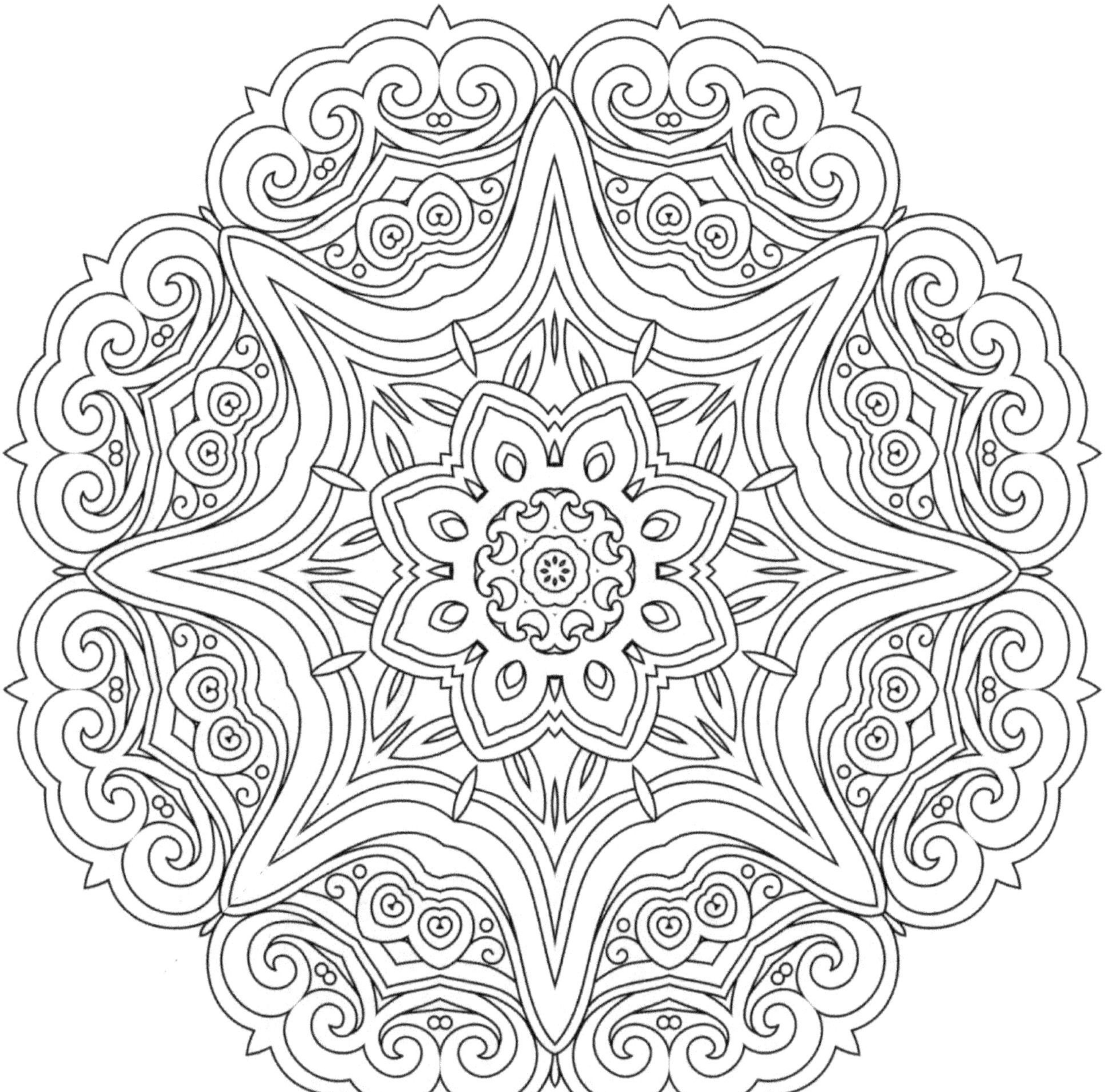

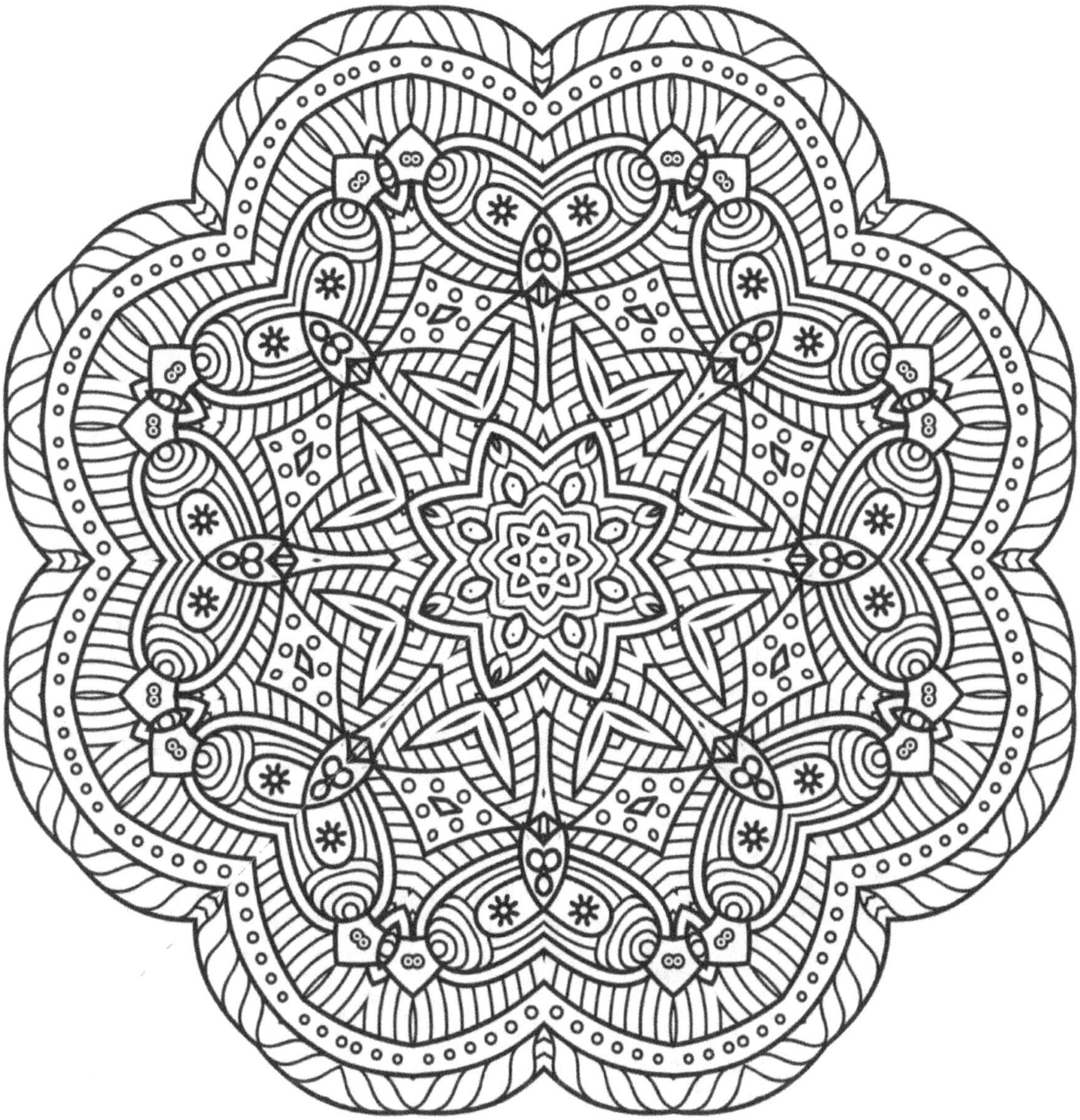

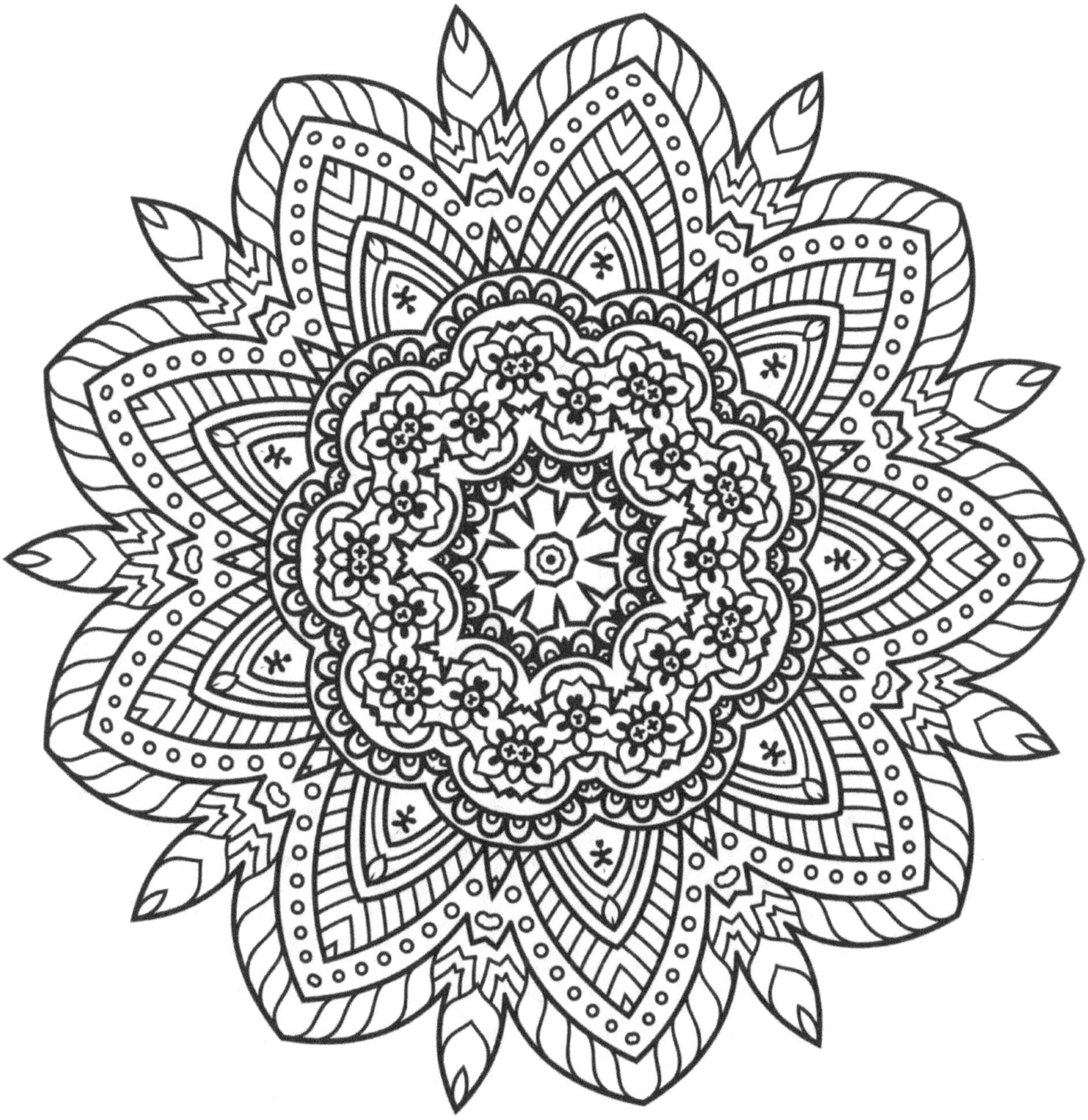

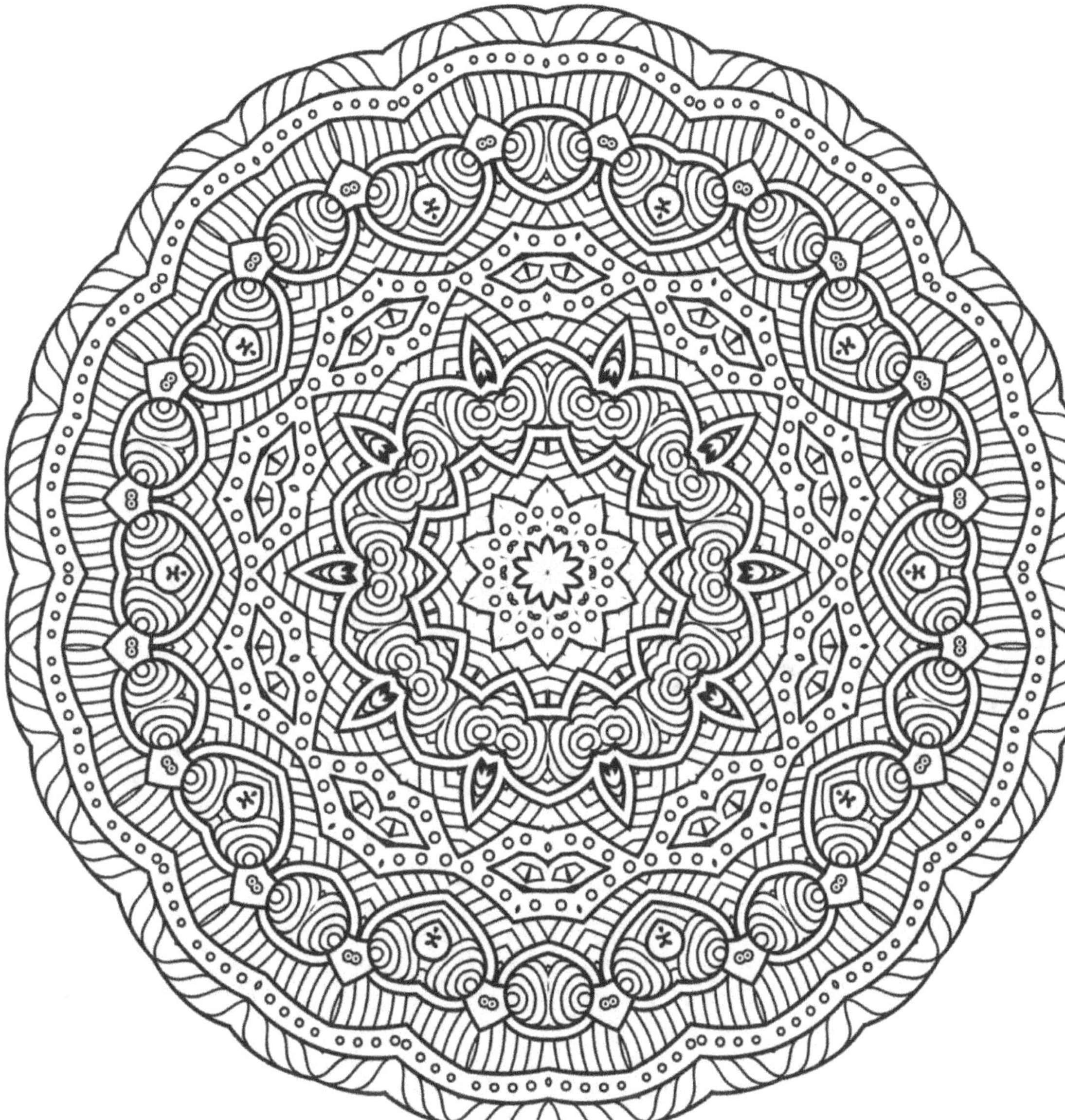

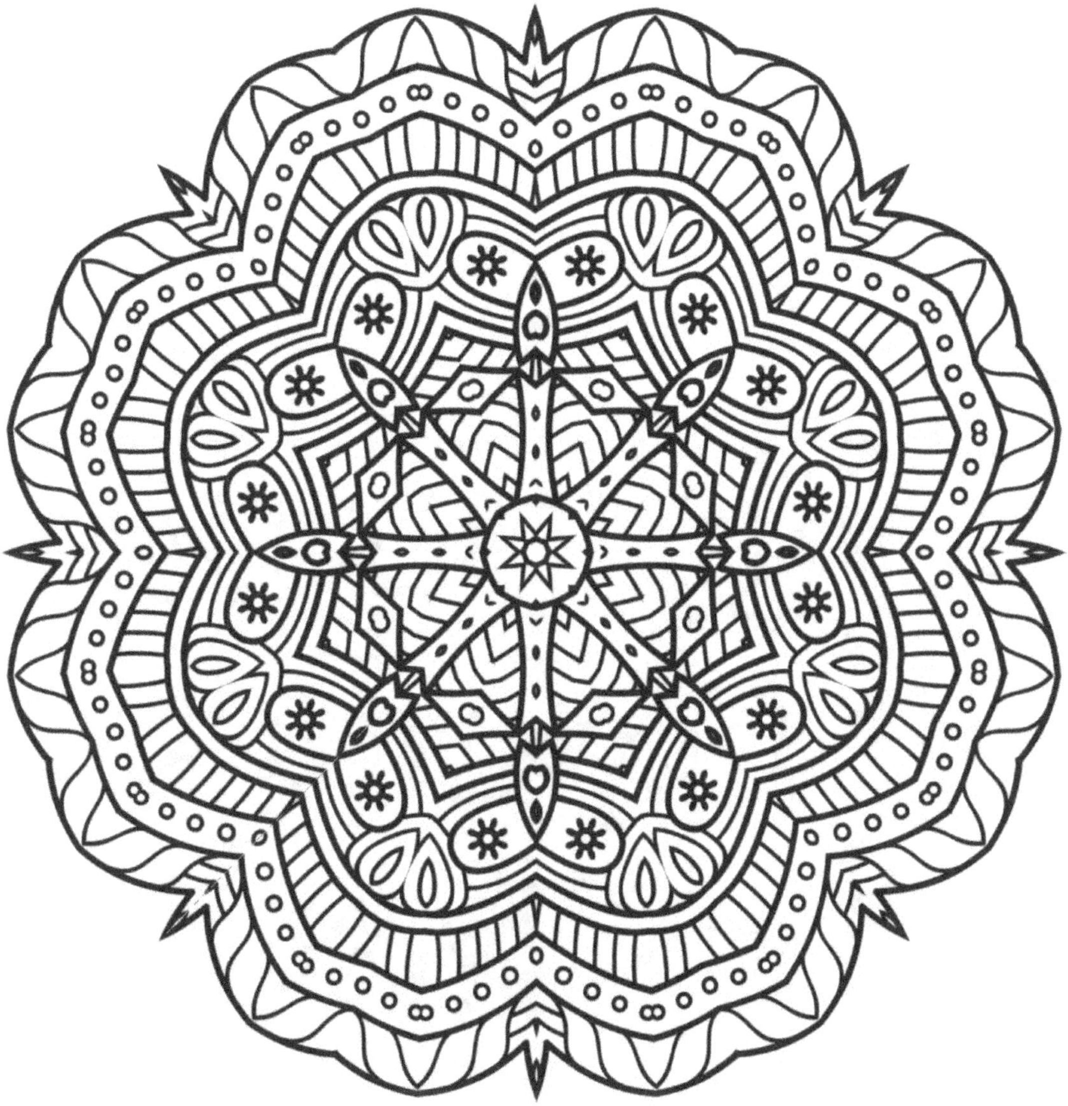

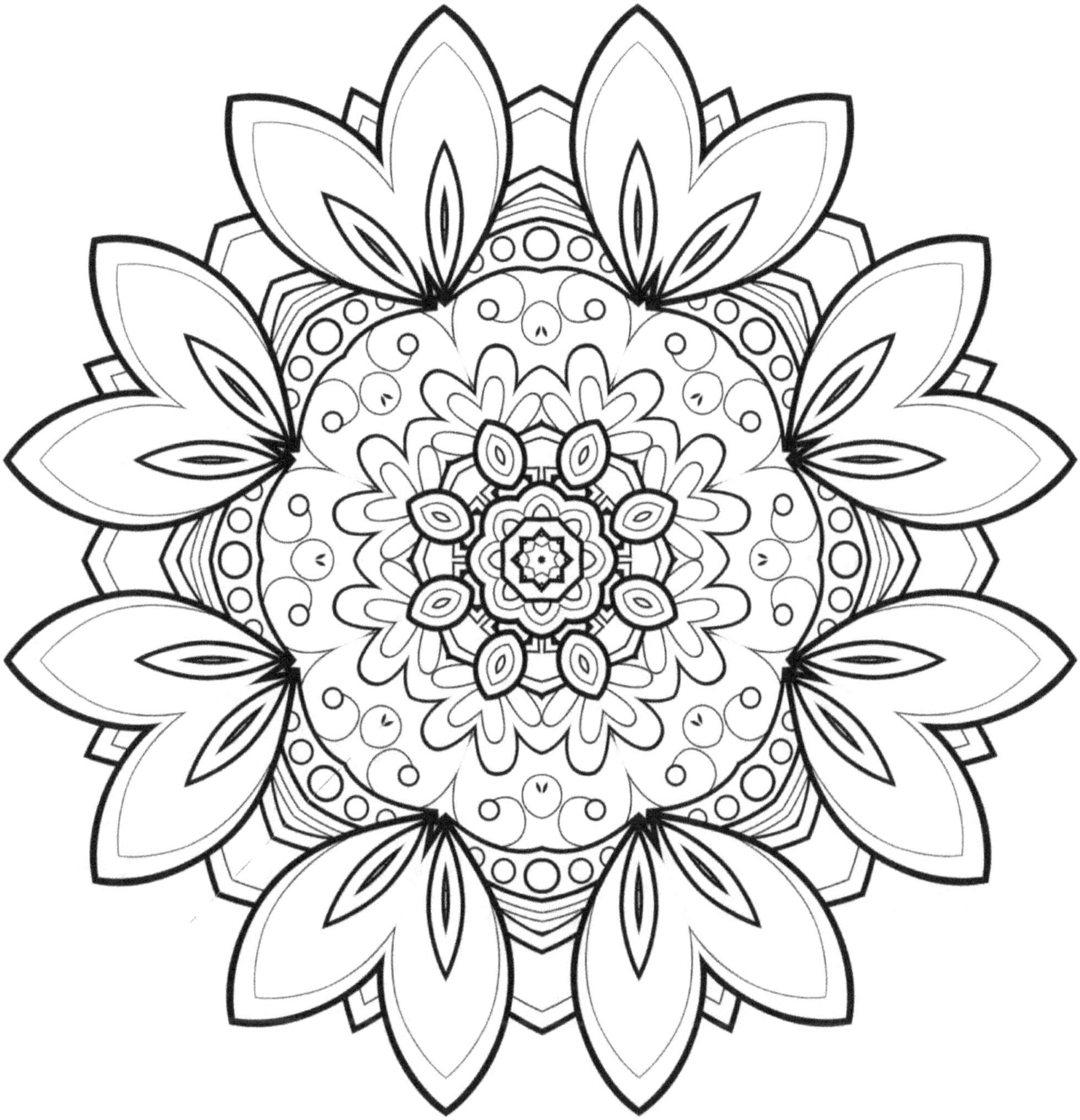

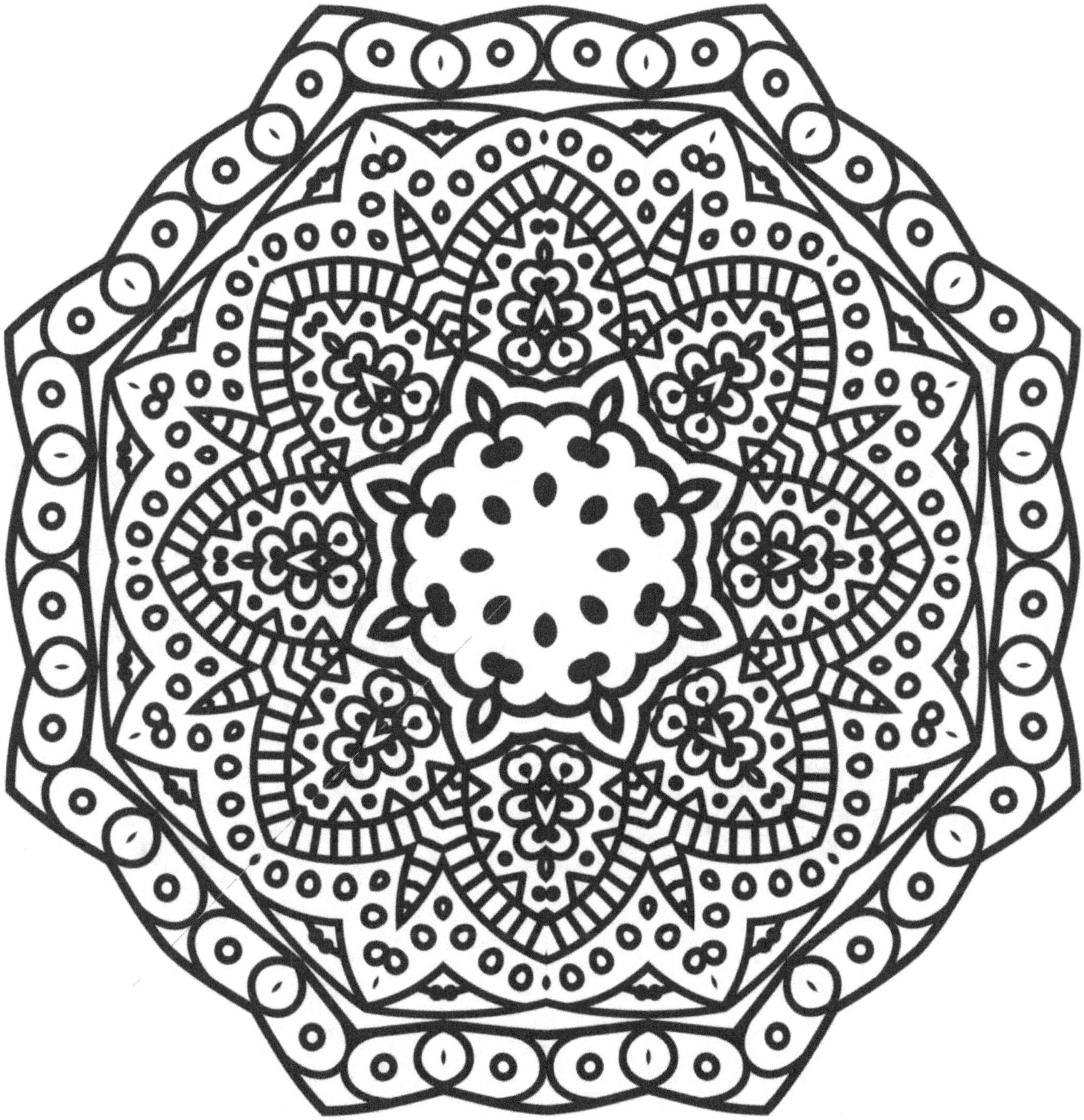

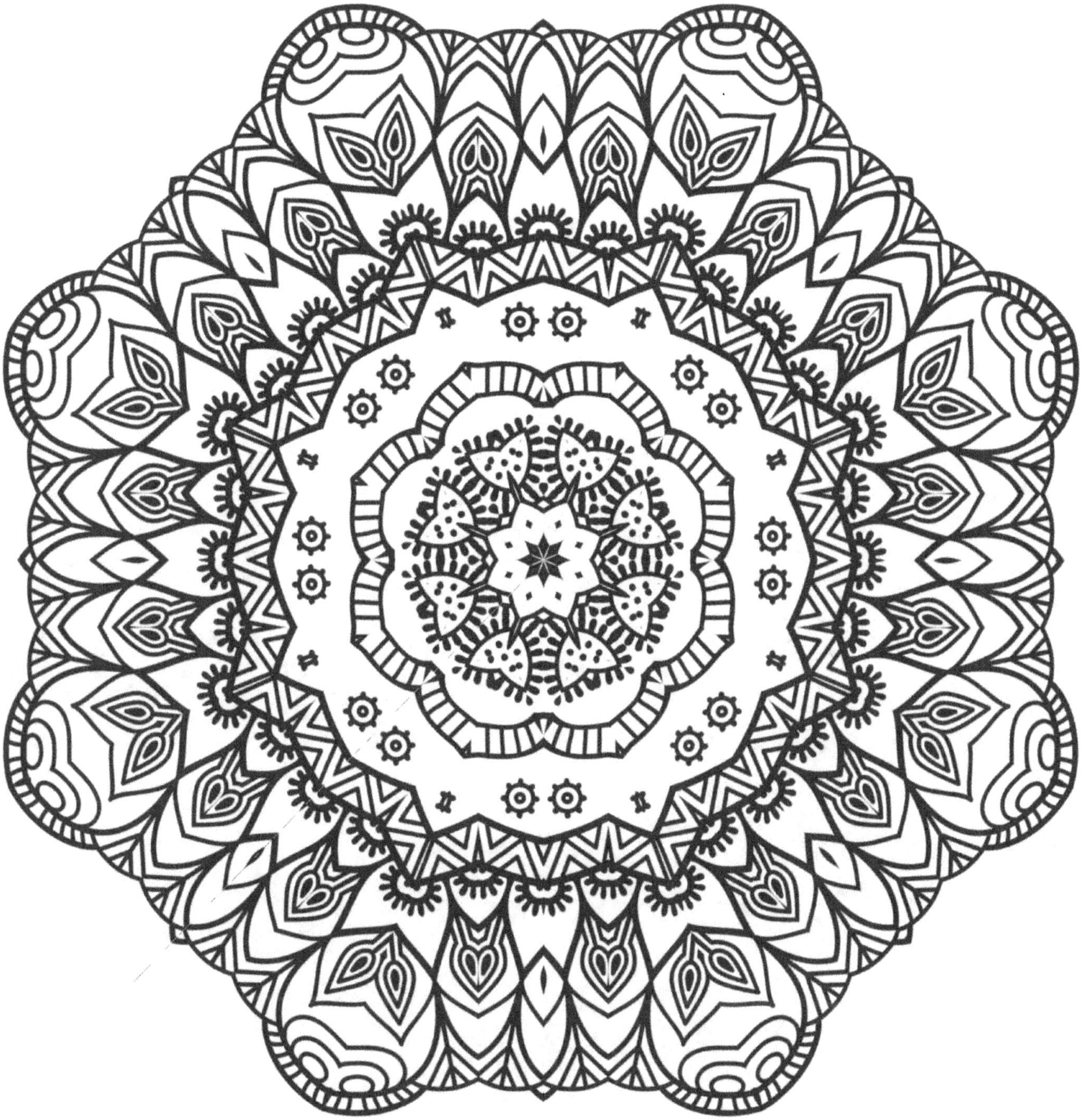

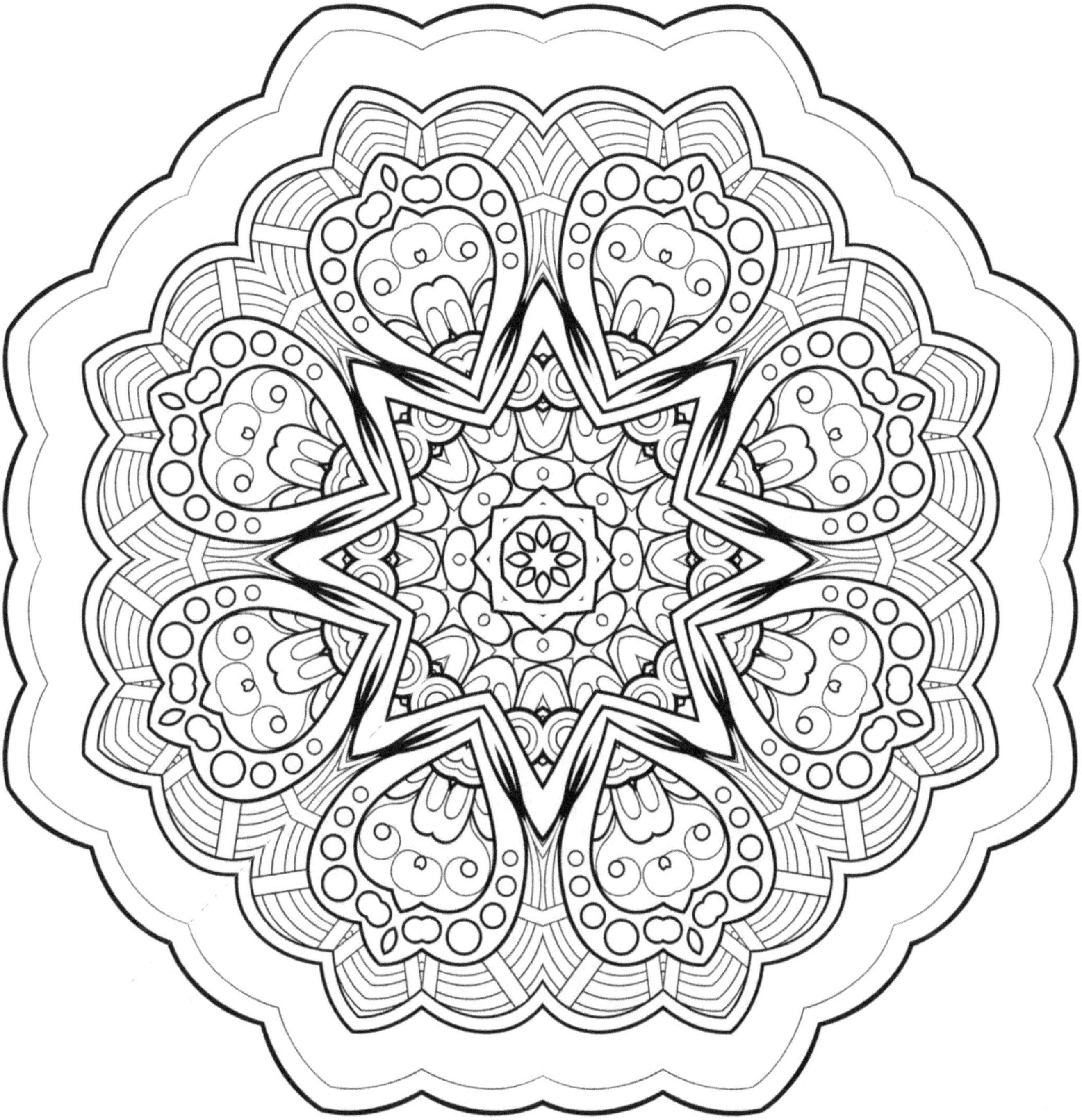

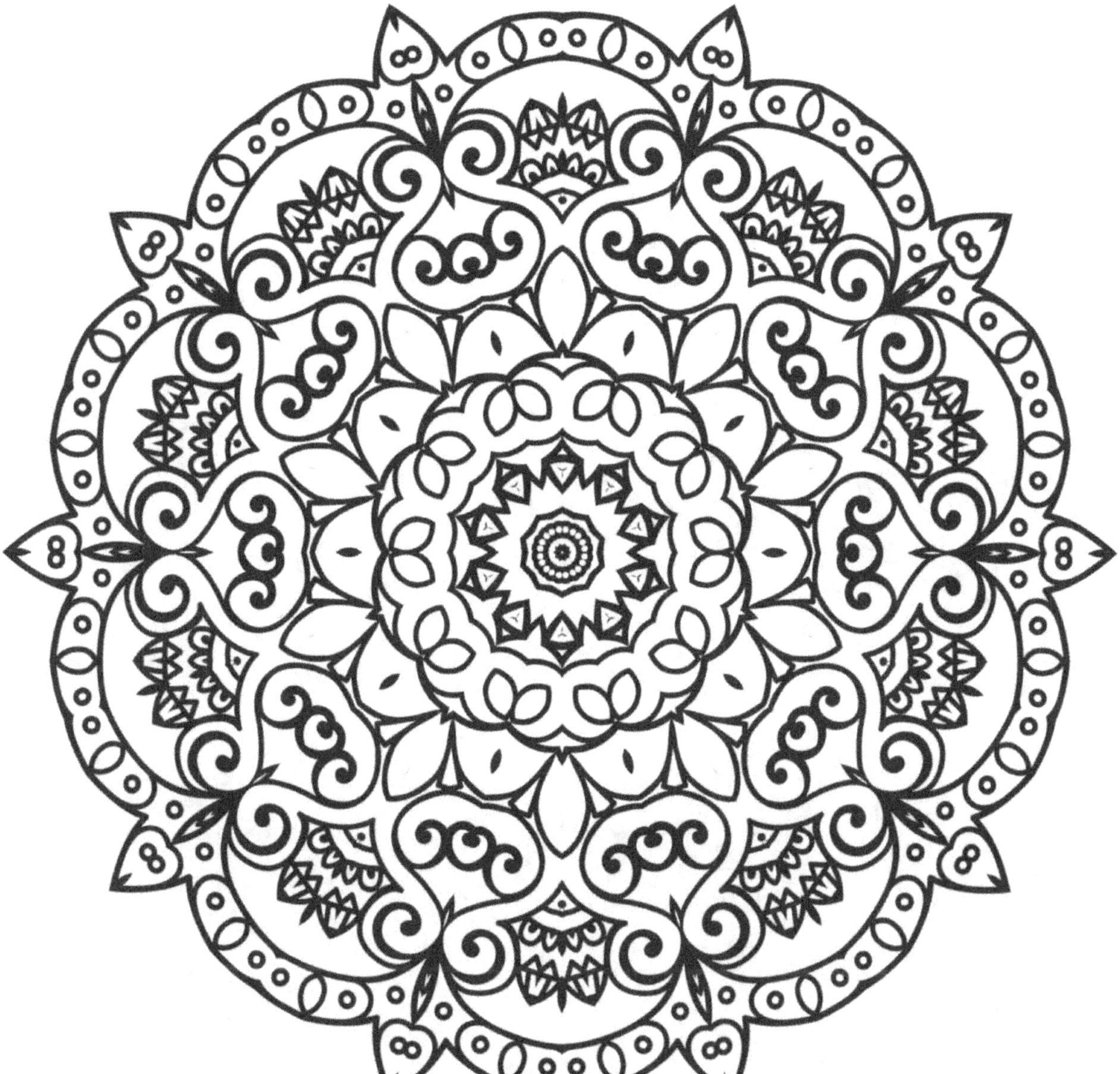

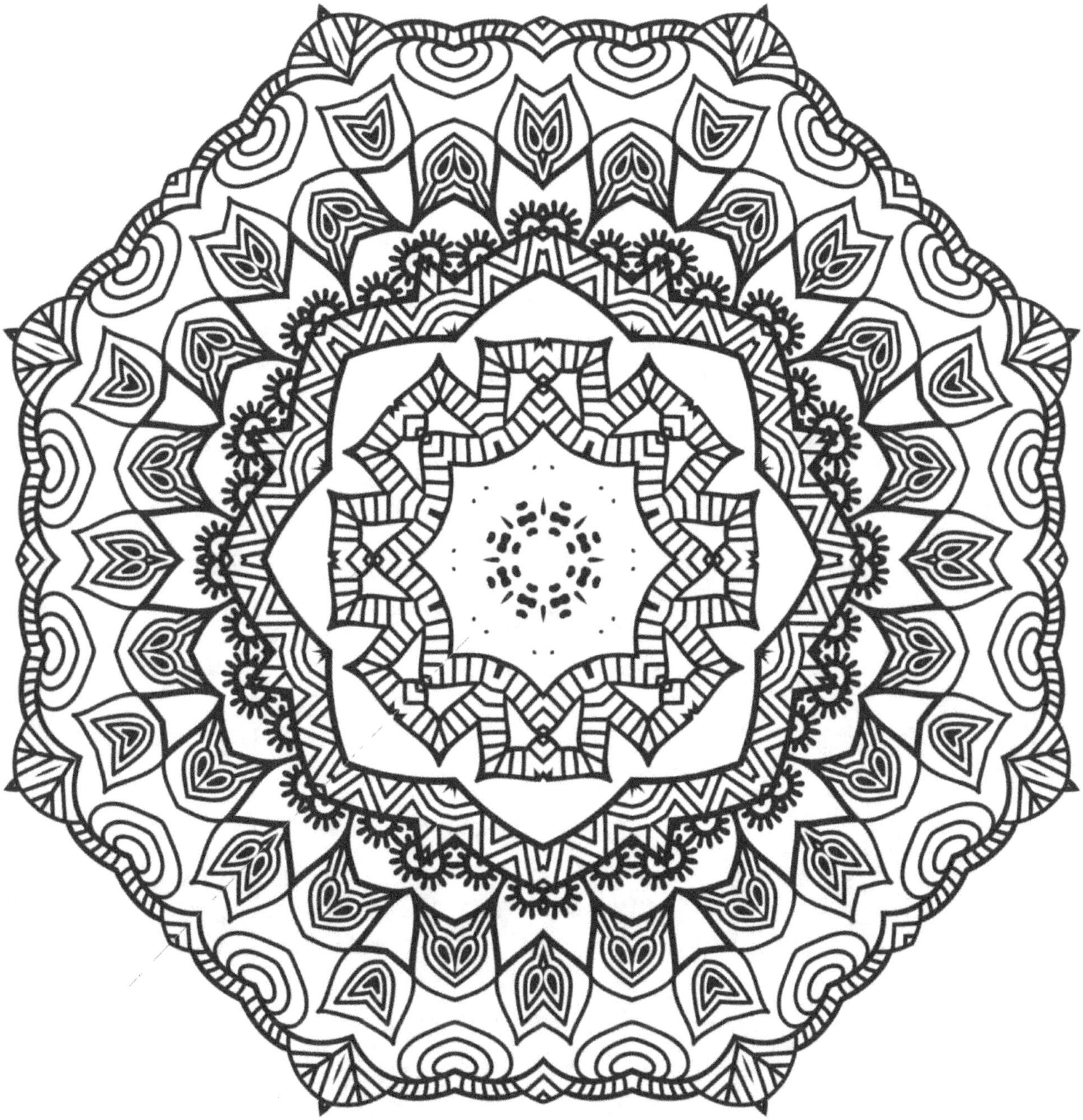

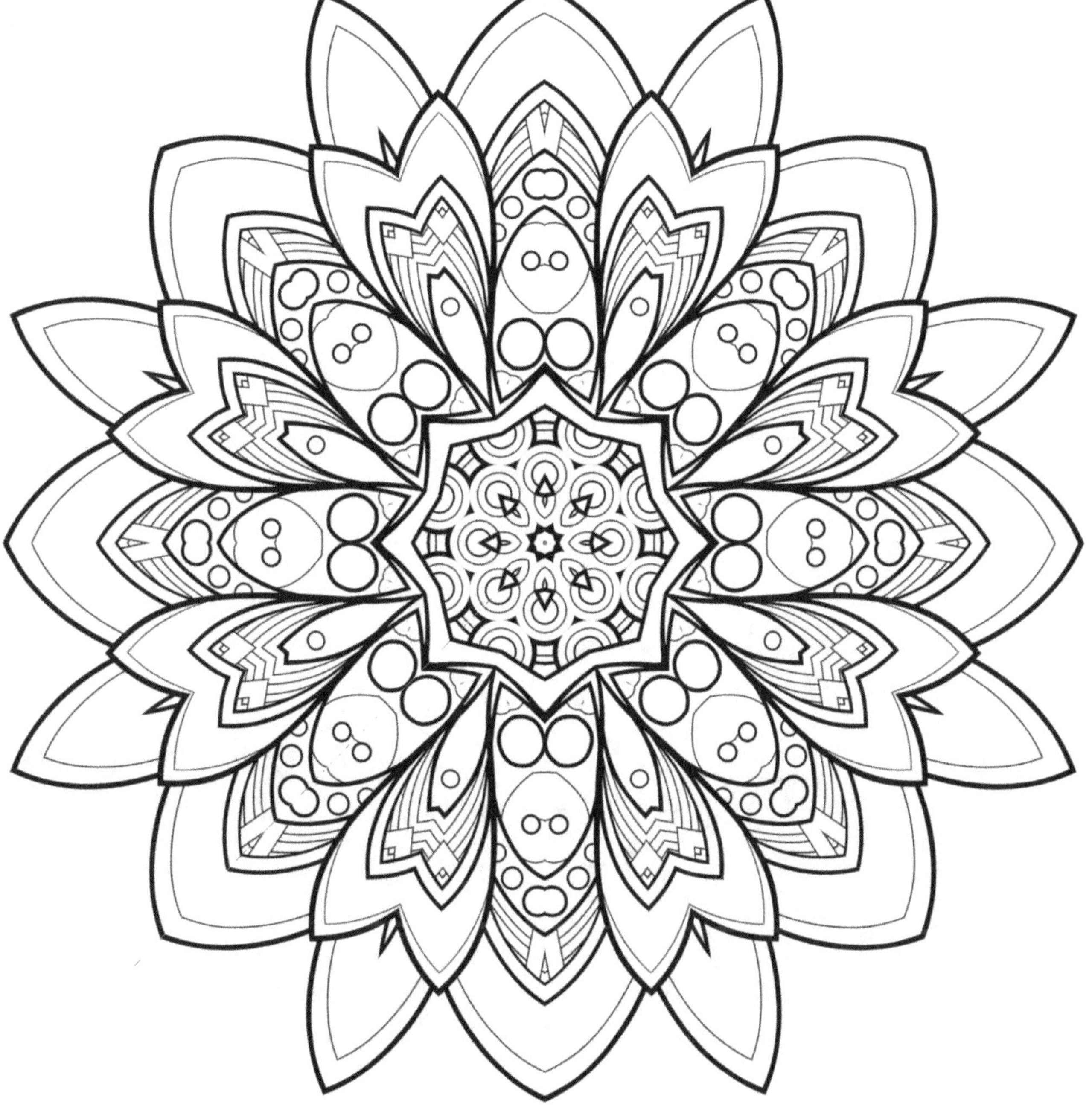

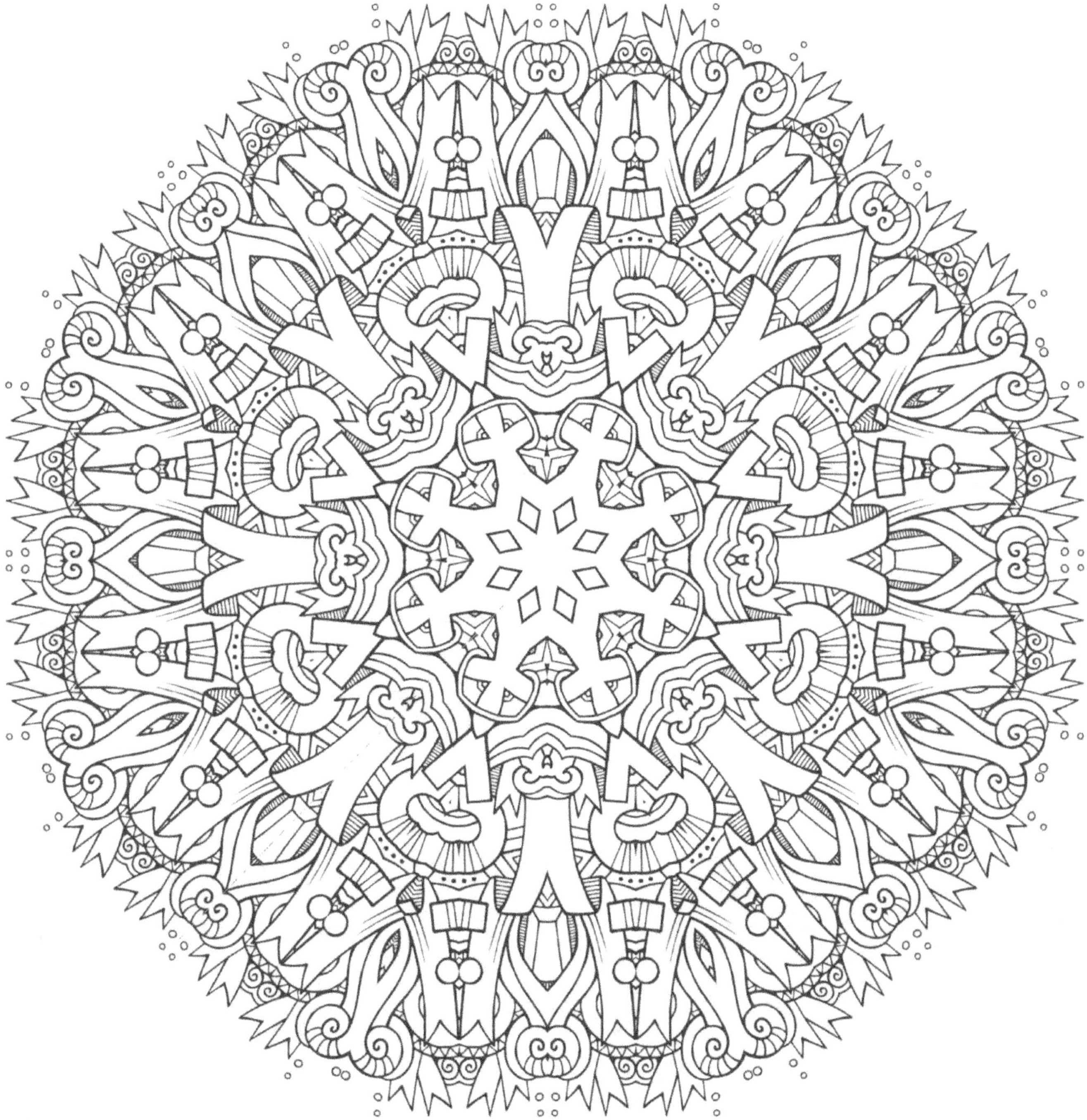

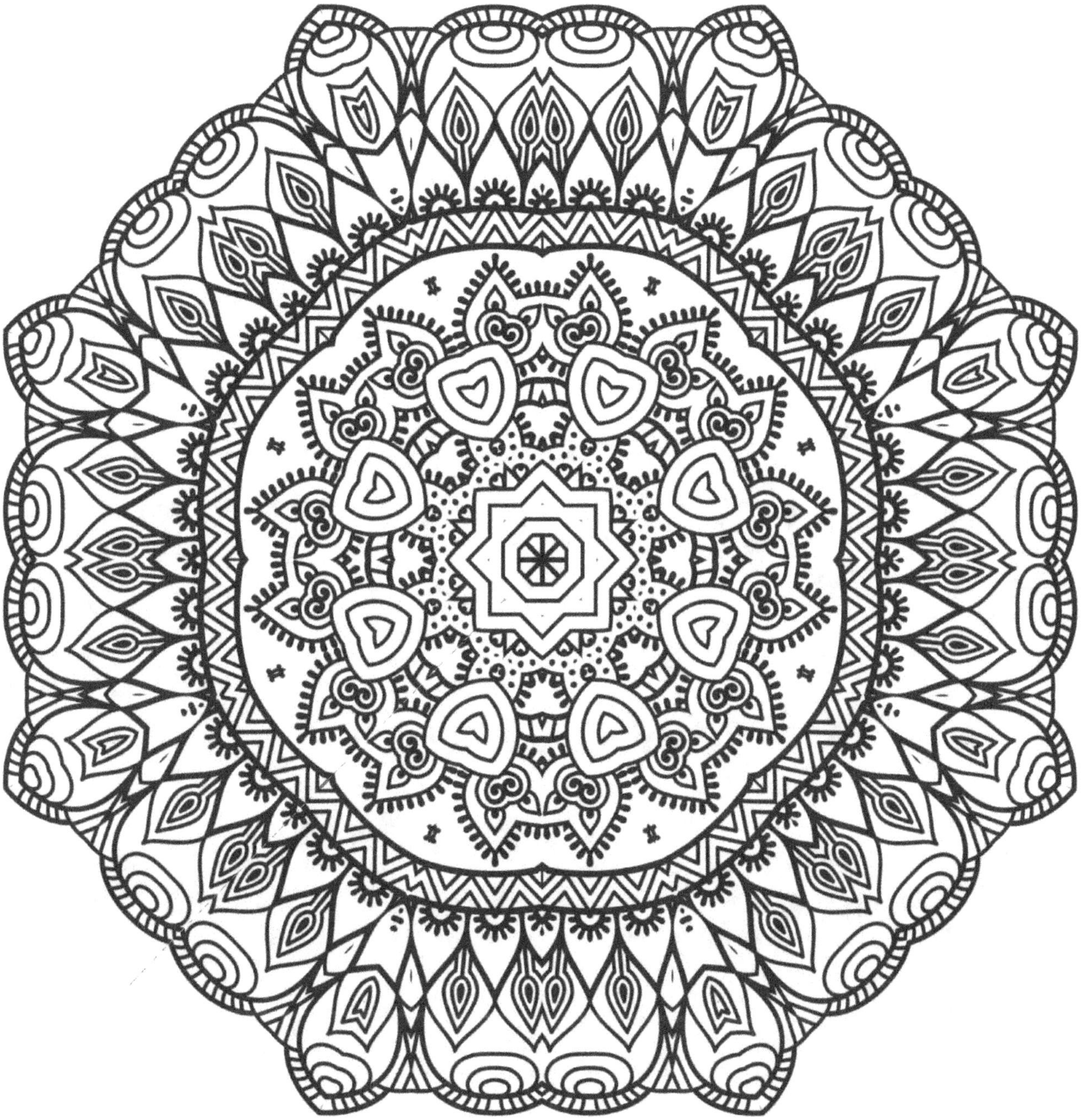

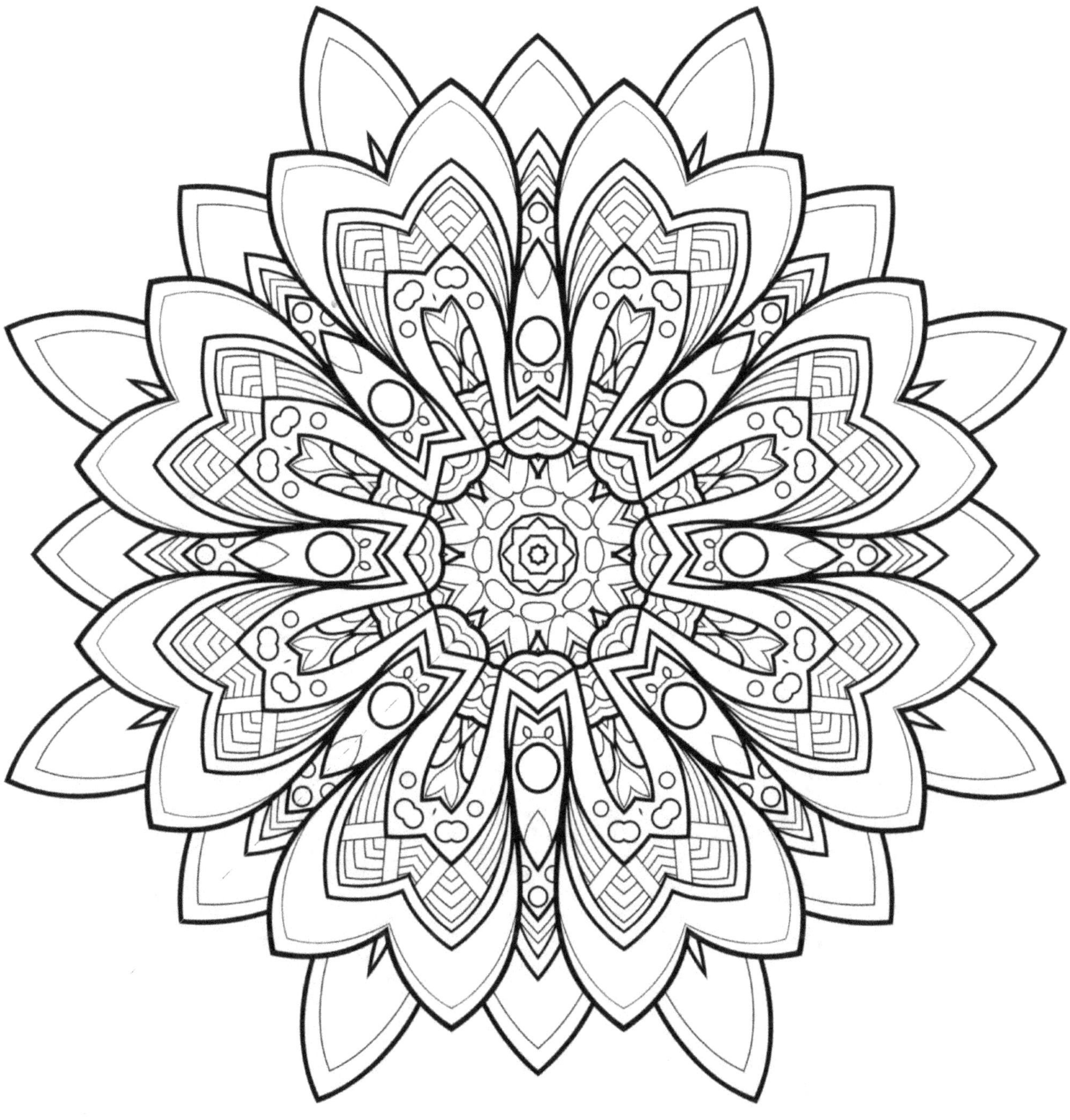

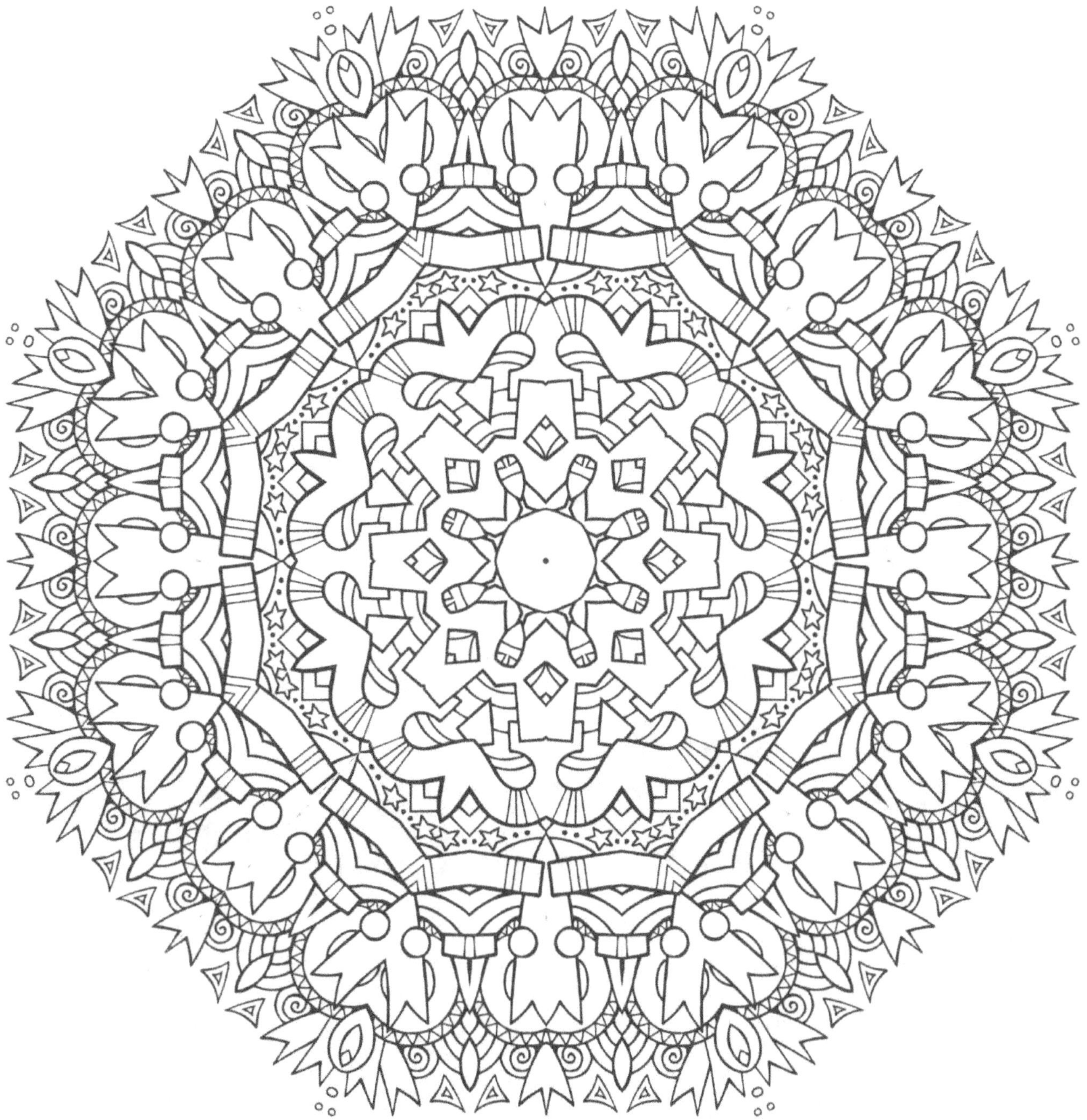

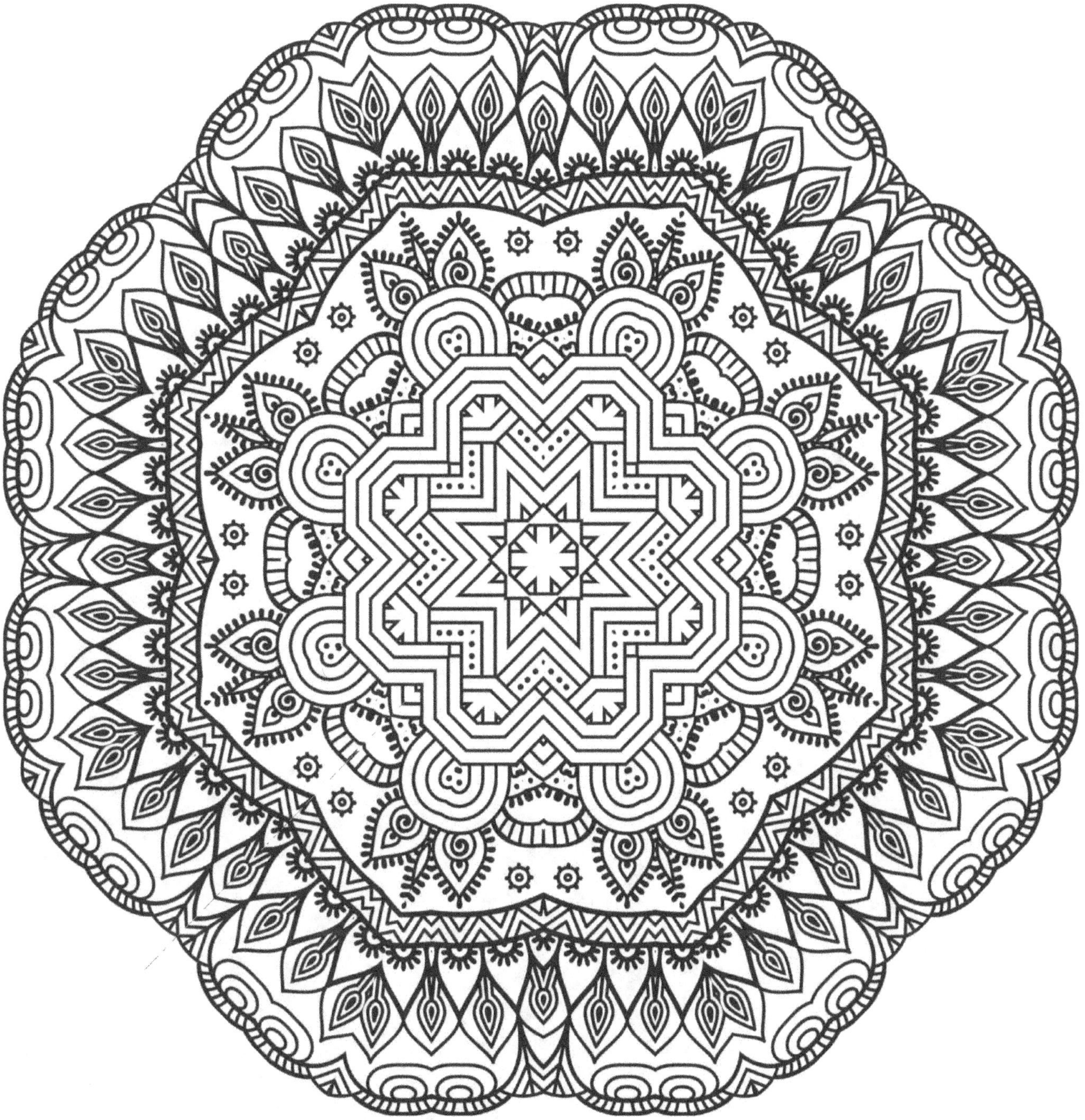

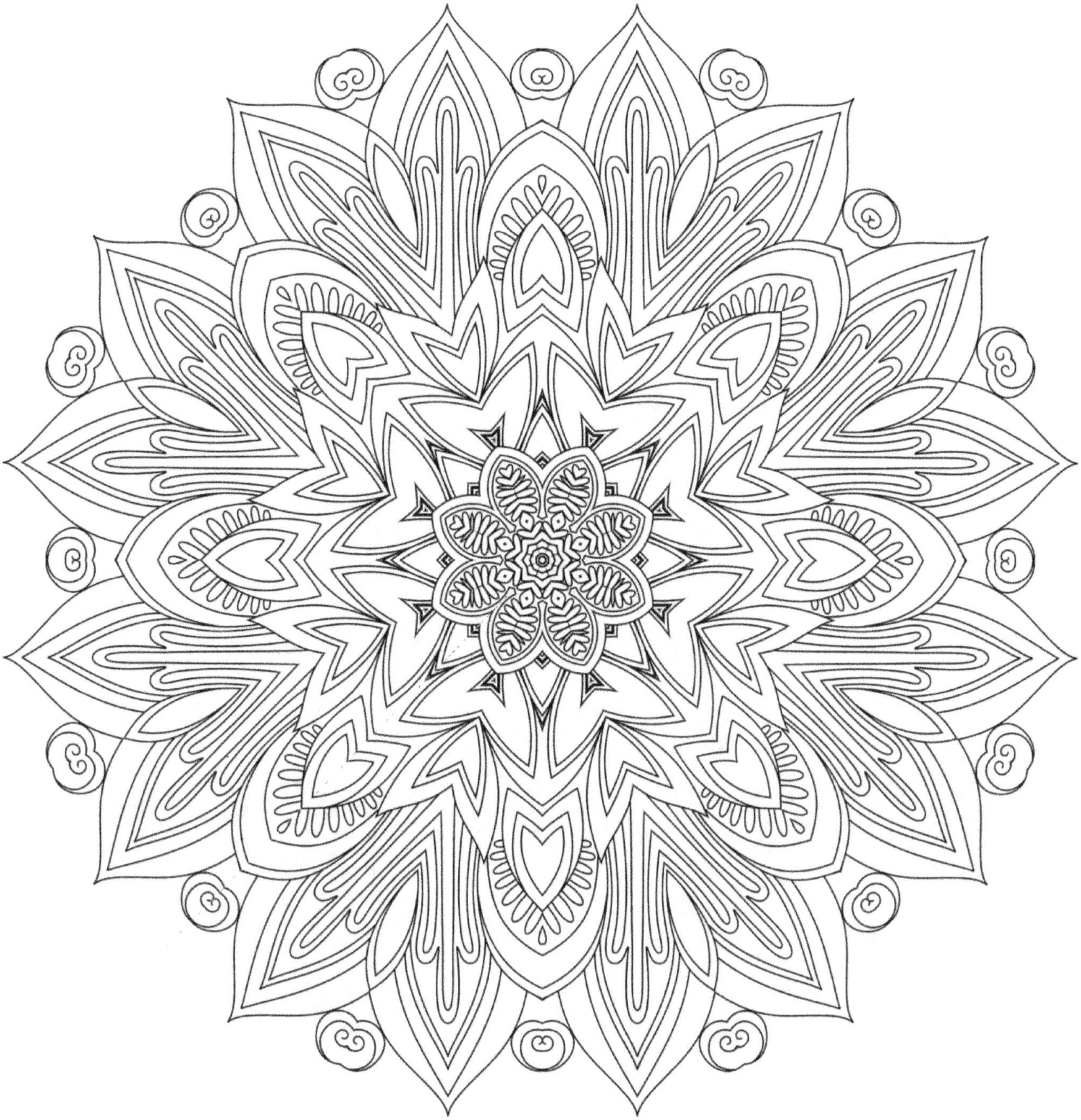

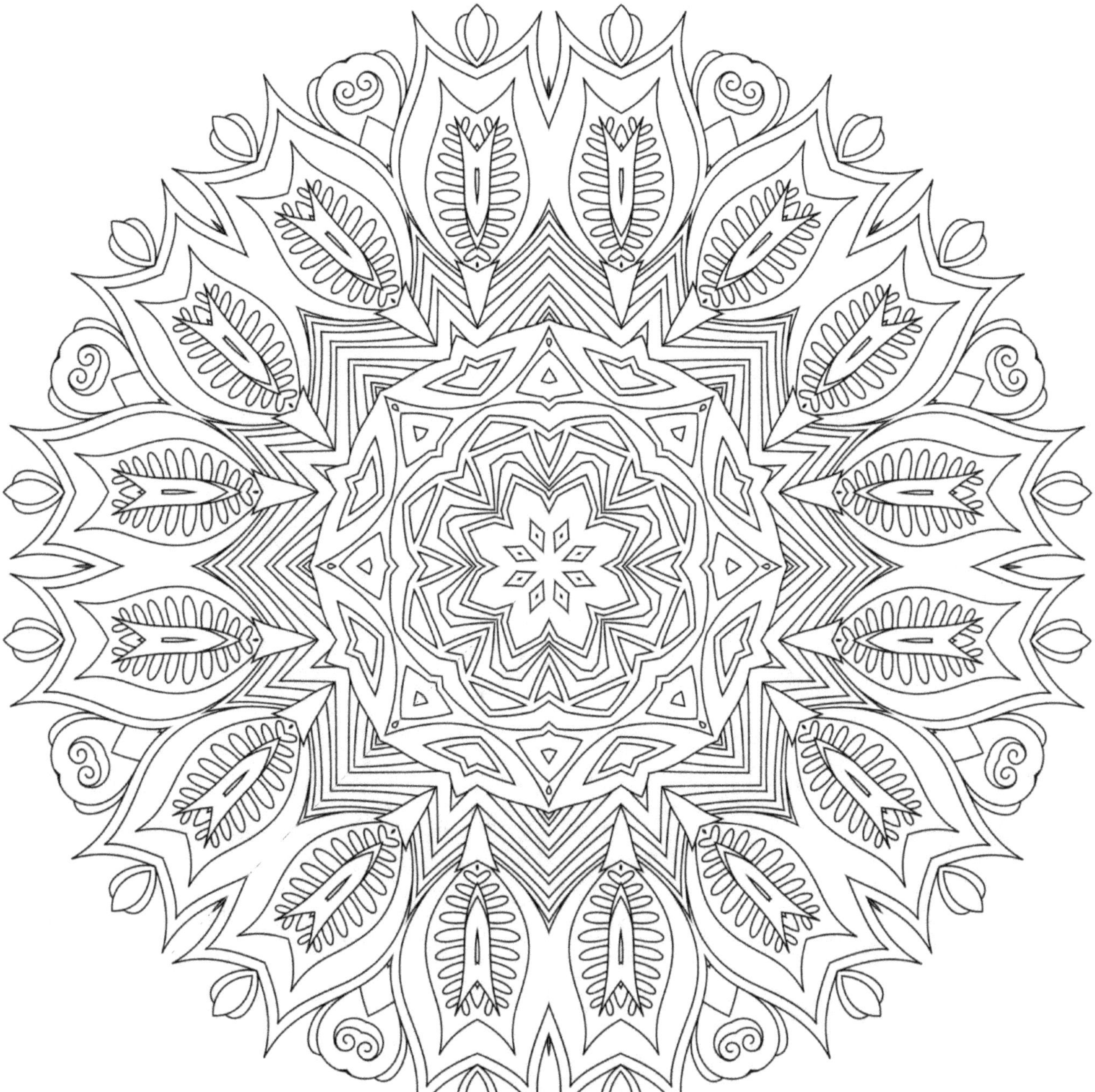

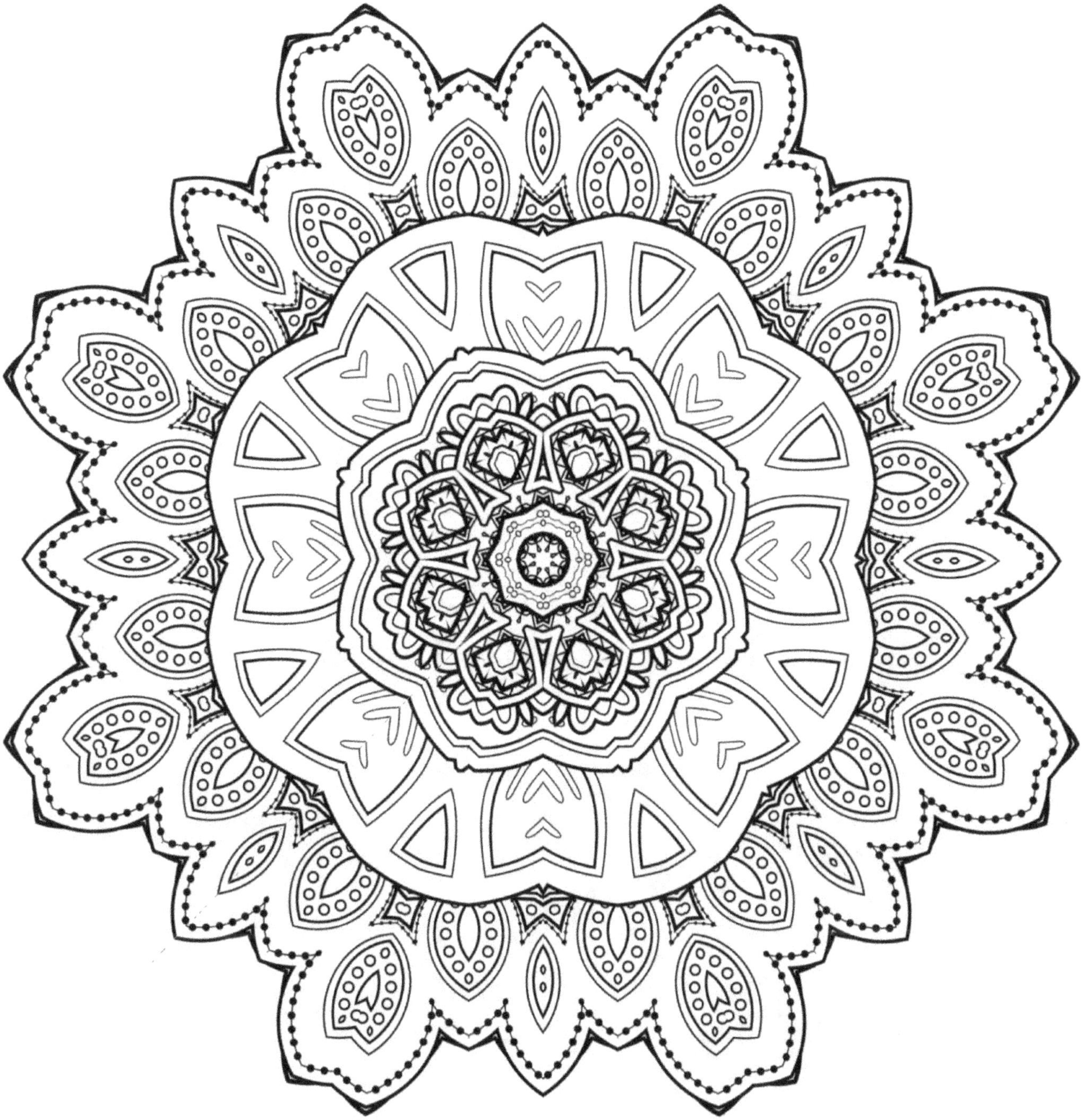

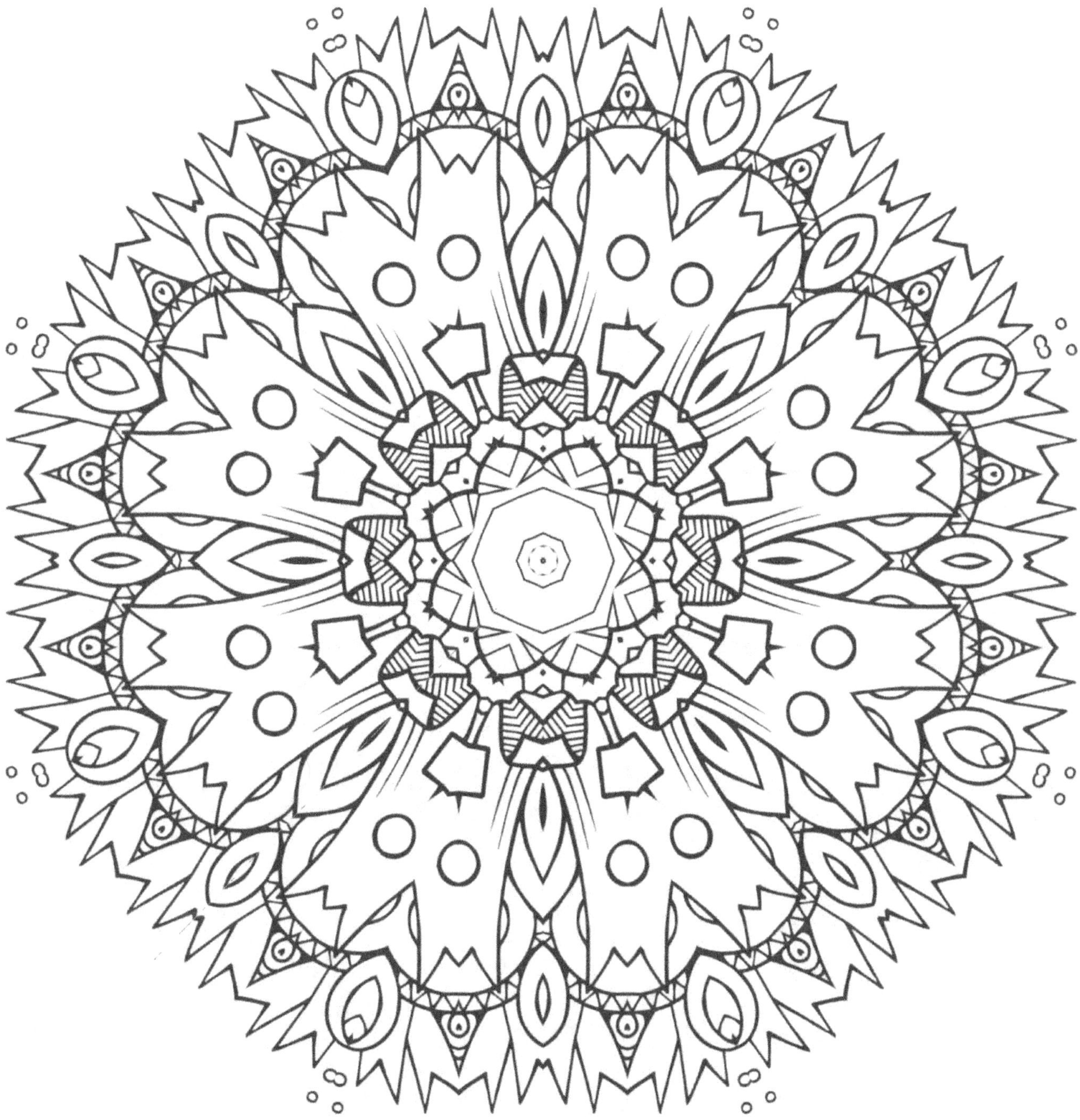

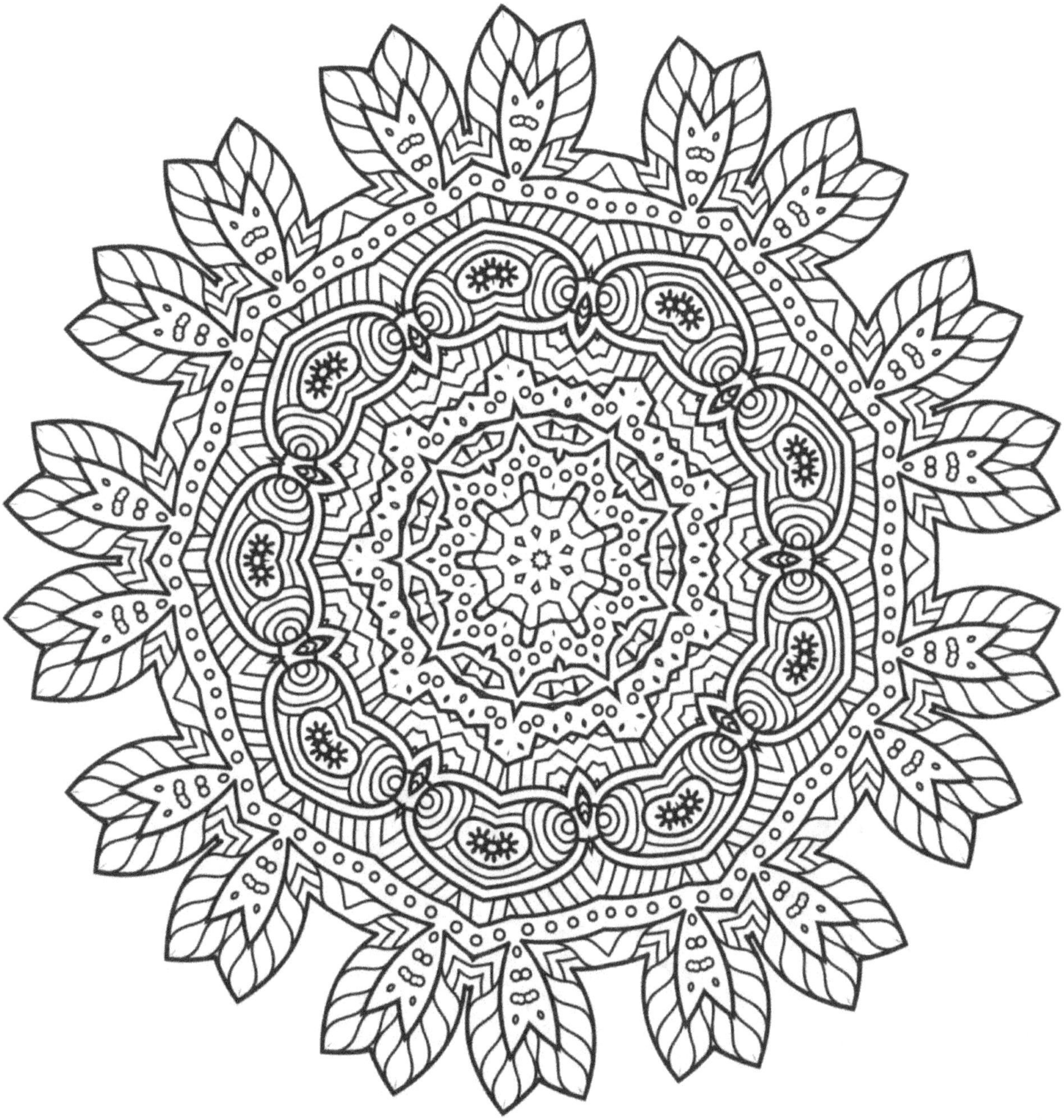

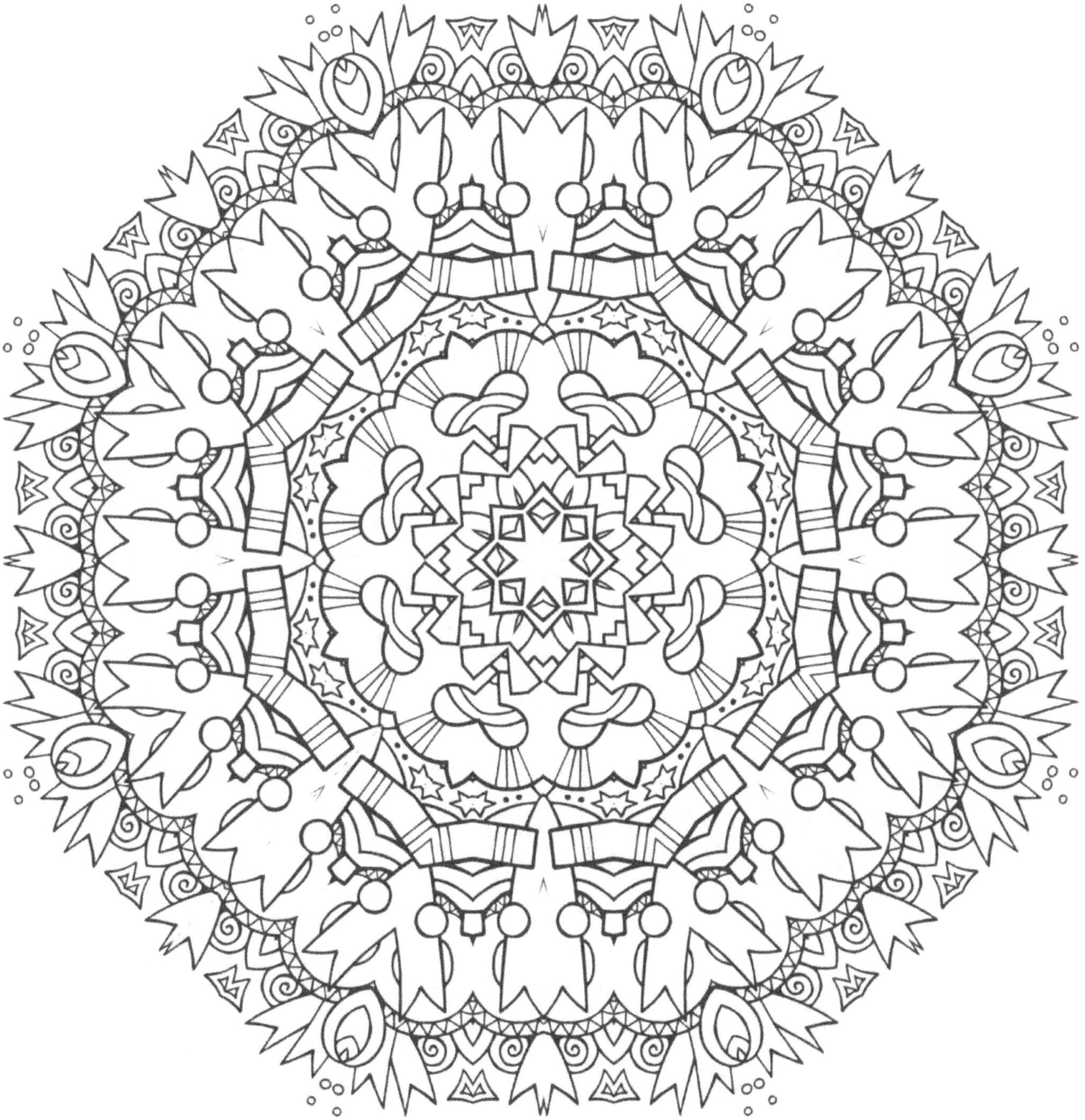

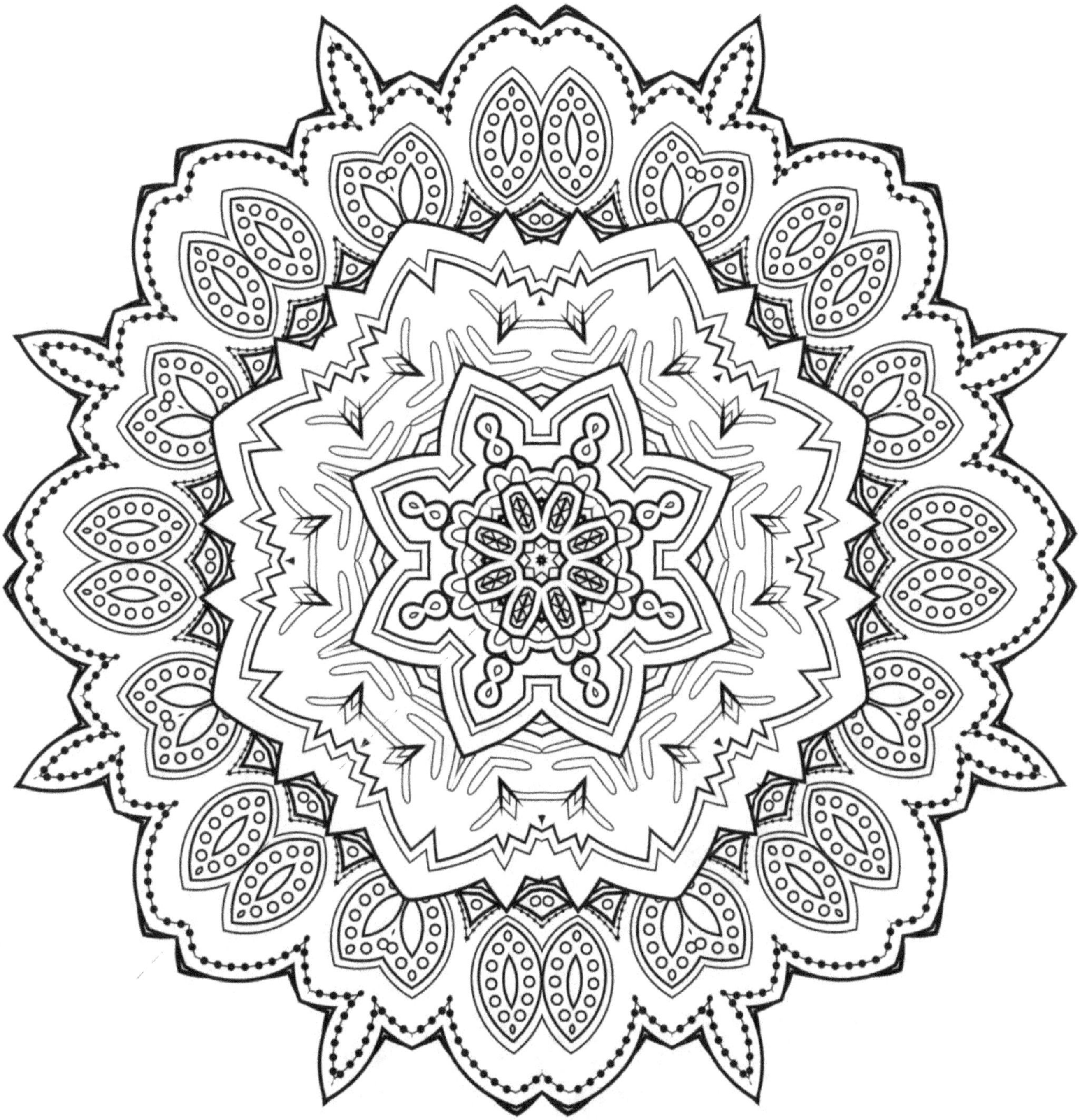

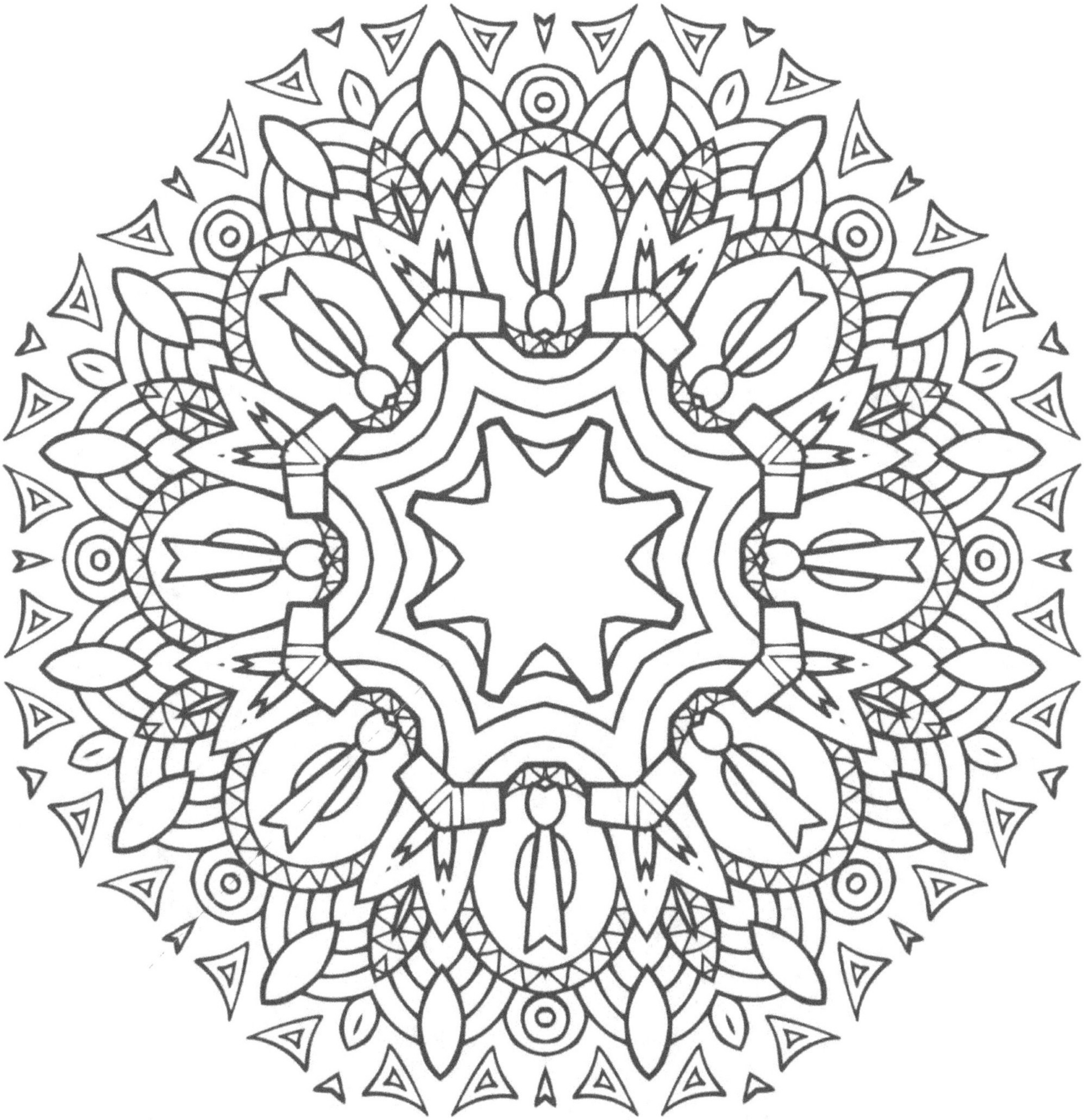

Hope you enjoy this coloring book.

Thank you.

www.ingramcontent.com/pod-product-compliance
Lightning Source LLC
Chambersburg PA
CBHW080834180526
45168CB00006B/2674
9781516972364